MALLORCA

TRAVEL GUIDE 2025-2026

JEFFREY J. BRITTAIN

TABLE OF CONTENTS

INTRODUCTION TO MALLORCA

CHAPTER 1: SOME ATTRACTIONS & MUST-SEE LANDMARKS

CHAPTER 2: RECOMMENDED BEACHES & COASTAL SPOTS

CHAPTER 3: OUTDOOR ADVENTURES & ACTIVITIES

CHAPTER 4: WHERE TO STAY (RECOMMENDED AREAS & BUDGET OPTIONS)

INTRODUCTION TO MALLORCA

I. OVERVIEW OF THE ISLAND

Mallorca, the largest of Spain's Balearic Islands, is a Mediterranean paradise known for its stunning coastline, diverse landscapes, rich history, and vibrant culture. Located off the eastern coast of Spain, Mallorca offers a unique blend of sun-soaked beaches, dramatic mountain ranges, and charming villages, making it a top destination for travelers seeking both relaxation and adventure.

The island is renowned for its breathtaking natural beauty, with over 550 kilometers of coastline featuring crystal-clear waters, sandy beaches, and secluded coves. From the famous Es Trenc beach with its Caribbean-like turquoise waters to the rugged cliffs of Sa Calobra, Mallorca's coastal scenery is diverse and picturesque. Inland, the island is dominated by the Serra de Tramuntana, a UNESCO World Heritage Site known for its dramatic peaks, winding roads, and traditional stone-built villages such as Valldemossa and

Deià. This mountain range is a paradise for hikers and cyclists, offering some of the trails in the Mediterranean.

Palma de Mallorca, the island's capital, is a dynamic city that seamlessly blends historic charm with modern amenities. The city's old town is a maze of narrow streets lined with Gothic architecture, bustling plazas, and hidden courtyards. Its most iconic landmark, La Seu Cathedral, is an awe-inspiring Gothic masterpiece overlooking the Bay of Palma. Beyond the cathedral, Palma offers a vibrant food scene, designer boutiques, and a lively nightlife, making it a cultural and entertainment hub.

Mallorca's history is deeply rooted in its strategic Mediterranean location, having been influenced by various civilizations, including the Romans, Moors, and Catalans. This rich heritage is reflected in the island's architecture, traditions, and cuisine. Historic sites such as Bellver Castle, the ruins of the Roman city of Pollentia, and the medieval town of Alcúdia offer glimpses into Mallorca's past, while local festivals and markets celebrate its enduring traditions.

The island's culinary scene is another highlight, with a mix of traditional Balearic flavors and modern gastronomic innovations.

Local specialties such as sobrasada (cured sausage), ensaïmada (a sweet pastry), and fresh seafood dishes reflect the island's agricultural and maritime heritage. Mallorca is also home to an emerging wine scene, with vineyards producing excellent local wines in regions such as Binissalem and Pla i Llevant.

Beyond its natural and cultural attractions, Mallorca offers a variety of outdoor activities, including sailing, snorkeling, golfing, and cycling. Its warm Mediterranean climate makes it a year-round destination, with hot summers for beach lovers and mild winters ideal for exploring the countryside and historical sites. Whether you're seeking adventure, relaxation, or cultural immersion, Mallorca provides a diverse and unforgettable experience for all types of travelers.

II. FAVOURABLE TIME TO VISIT

The favourable time to visit Mallorca depends on what kind of experience you are looking for, as the island offers distinct seasonal advantages throughout the year. Thanks to its Mediterranean climate, Mallorca enjoys warm summers, mild winters, and pleasant spring and autumn seasons, making it a year-round destination. However, certain months are more favorable depending on whether you want to enjoy beach relaxation, outdoor adventures, or cultural exploration.

For travelers looking to experience Mallorca's famous beaches, the summer months from **June to August** are the most popular. During this period, the island enjoys long sunny days with temperatures averaging between 25°C and 35°C (77°F to 95°F), making it for swimming, sunbathing, and water sports. The sea is warm and inviting, and all beachside resorts, restaurants, and nightlife venues are in full swing. However, summer is also the busiest season, attracting large crowds, especially in tourist hotspots such as Palma, Magaluf, and Alcúdia. Prices for accommodation and flights are at their peak, so early booking is recommended.

If you prefer a more tranquil and comfortable experience, **spring (March to May) and autumn (September to November)** are ideal seasons to visit Mallorca. During spring, the island bursts into life with colorful wildflowers, blossoming almond trees, and pleasant daytime temperatures ranging between 17°C and 25°C (63°F to 77°F). This is an excellent time for hiking, cycling, and exploring the scenic villages in the Tramuntana Mountains without the intense heat of summer. Autumn is equally beautiful, with warm sea temperatures lingering from the summer, making it possible to enjoy the beaches while avoiding the peak-season crowds. September, in particular, is a fantastic time to visit as the island is still lively, but accommodation prices begin to drop.

For those interested in outdoor activities such as hiking, cycling, and sightseeing, **winter (December to February)** offers a completely different but equally rewarding experience. The island's temperatures range from 10°C to 18°C (50°F to 64°F), providing cool but comfortable conditions for exploring historic towns, wine regions, and cultural landmarks. Winter is the quietest season, meaning fewer tourists, lower prices, and a more authentic experience. Palma, in particular, comes to life with Christmas markets, festive lights, and traditional celebrations. However, beachgoers might find winter less appealing as the sea is cooler, and some beachside restaurants and resorts temporarily close.

Essentially, the most favorable time to visit Mallorca depends on personal preferences. For a lively beach vacation and nightlife, summer is the choice. If you prefer a balance between good weather and fewer crowds, spring and autumn are . For cultural exploration and outdoor adventures in a peaceful setting, winter offers a unique side of the island.

III. HOW TO GET THERE

Getting to Mallorca is straightforward, as the island is well-connected to major cities in Europe and beyond through air and sea travel. As the largest island in the Balearic archipelago, Mallorca has a modern international airport, efficient ferry services, and a variety of transportation options for travelers arriving from different parts of the world.

The **primary gateway to Mallorca** is **Palma de Mallorca Airport (PMI)**, also known as **Son Sant Joan Airport**, located about 8 kilometers east of Palma, the island's capital. This airport is the third busiest in Spain, handling millions of passengers each year, especially during the peak summer season. It is well-equipped with modern facilities, duty-free shops, restaurants, and car rental services. PMI serves a vast network of airlines, including both full-service carriers and budget airlines, making it an accessible destination for travelers of all budgets.

Flights to Mallorca are frequent from major European cities such as London, Berlin, Paris, Madrid, Barcelona, Amsterdam, and Rome. Many airlines, including Iberia, Ryanair, Vueling, Lufthansa, and EasyJet, operate direct flights, with travel times typically ranging between 1 to 3 hours from most European hubs. For long-haul travelers from North America, Asia, or Australia, reaching Mallorca often involves a layover in a major European city such as Madrid, Barcelona, or Frankfurt before connecting to a short-haul flight to Palma.

For those who prefer traveling by sea, Mallorca is accessible via ferries from mainland Spain. Regular ferry services operate between **Mallorca and cities like Barcelona, Valencia, and Dénia**, providing an alternative to air travel. These ferries, operated by companies such as **Balearia, Trasmed, and Grandi Navi Veloci (GNV)**, offer a range of options from fast ferries, which take about 3-4 hours, to overnight crossings on larger vessels equipped with cabins and dining facilities. The primary ferry port in Mallorca is

Port de Palma, situated in Palma de Mallorca, with additional ports in Alcúdia, which mainly serves routes to Menorca.

For travelers coming from other Balearic Islands, ferry connections are available from **Ibiza, Menorca, and Formentera**. These routes are particularly convenient for those planning to explore multiple islands, as high-speed ferries make inter-island travel efficient. The ferry journey from Ibiza to Mallorca takes approximately 2 to 3 hours, while the route from Menorca to Mallorca is slightly shorter, at around 1.5 to 2 hours.

Upon arrival in Mallorca, transportation from the airport or ferry terminals to various destinations on the island is efficient and well-organized. Taxis, rental cars, and buses are readily available at the airport, providing easy access to Palma and other major towns. The **A1 bus service** connects the airport to Palma city center in about 15 minutes, offering an affordable and convenient option. For those staying in more remote areas of the island, renting a car is highly recommended, as it provides the flexibility to explore Mallorca's scenic landscapes, hidden beaches, and charming villages at your own pace.

While air travel is the fastest and most convenient way to reach Mallorca, taking a ferry can be a scenic and enjoyable experience, especially for those traveling with a vehicle or looking to combine their visit with other Spanish coastal destinations. Regardless of the mode of transport, reaching Mallorca is easy, with multiple options catering to different travel preferences.

IV. VISA REQUIREMENTS & ENTRY REGULATIONS

VISA REQUIREMENTS

Mallorca, as part of Spain and the Schengen Area, follows standard **Schengen visa regulations** for international travelers. The specific visa requirements depend on the traveler's nationality, the purpose of the visit, and the duration of stay. Citizens of the **European Union (EU), European Economic Area (EEA), and Switzerland** do not require a visa to enter Mallorca, as they can travel freely within the Schengen Zone with just a valid national ID card or passport.

For **non-EU travelers**, different rules apply. Visitors from **Schengen visa-exempt countries**, including the **United States, Canada, the United Kingdom, Australia, New Zealand, Japan,**

and South Korea, can enter Mallorca for up to **90 days within a 180-day period** without a visa. This allows for tourism, business, or family visits, but employment or long-term stays require a specific visa or residency permit.

Travelers from countries **not on the visa-exempt list** must obtain a **Schengen visa** before arriving in Mallorca. This visa allows entry into all Schengen countries for a maximum of **90 days within a 180-day period**. The application must be submitted at a **Spanish consulate or embassy** in the traveler's home country. Requirements typically include a **completed visa application form, passport valid for at least three months beyond the intended stay, proof of accommodation, travel itinerary, travel insurance covering a minimum of €30,000 in medical expenses, and proof of financial means** (such as bank statements or a sponsorship letter).

For those planning to stay in Mallorca beyond 90 days, a **long-term visa or residence permit** is necessary. This applies to students, workers, retirees, or individuals looking to establish residency. Applicants must follow specific procedures at the Spanish consulate, and requirements vary depending on the purpose of the stay.

As of **2025**, travelers from visa-exempt countries will be required to obtain an **ETIAS (European Travel Information and Authorization System)** approval before entering Spain. ETIAS is an online pre-travel authorization similar to the U.S. ESTA system, aimed at enhancing border security. It will be mandatory for travelers who do not need a Schengen visa and will require an online application, a small fee, and approval before boarding a flight or ferry to Mallorca.

ENTRY REGULATIONS

To enter Mallorca, travelers must comply with Spanish border regulations, including **passport validity, customs rules, and health requirements**. Regardless of visa requirements, all visitors must have a **valid passport or national ID card**. For non-EU travelers, the passport must be **valid for at least three months beyond the intended departure date** from the Schengen Zone.

Upon arrival, visitors may be asked to provide **proof of sufficient funds**, a **return or onward travel ticket**, and **confirmation of**

accommodation (hotel booking, rental agreement, or invitation letter from a host). While these checks are not always enforced, border officers have the right to request them, especially for travelers without a visa.

Spain follows standard **Schengen border control procedures**, meaning that EU/EEA/Swiss citizens can enter Mallorca without passport checks if arriving from another Schengen country. However, non-EU travelers are subject to entry stamps and border control checks.

Regarding **customs regulations**, Spain enforces limits on the amount of alcohol, tobacco, and cash that can be brought into the country. Travelers carrying more than **€10,000 in cash** (or equivalent in another currency) must declare it upon entry. Restricted and prohibited items include **illegal drugs, weapons, and certain agricultural products** to prevent the spread of pests and diseases.

In terms of **health regulations**, there are currently no COVID-19-related entry restrictions, but travelers should always check for updates before departure. Spain may require proof of vaccination, negative test results, or health declarations in response to global health concerns. Additionally, **travelers from certain countries must show proof of yellow fever vaccination** if they have recently visited high-risk areas.

For pet owners traveling with animals, Spain follows EU **pet travel regulations**, requiring microchipping, rabies vaccination, and a pet passport for dogs, cats, and ferrets. Non-EU pet owners should check the specific requirements before travel to ensure compliance.

Understanding visa and entry regulations in advance ensures a smooth arrival in Mallorca, preventing delays or travel disruptions at the border.

V. CURRENCY & BUDGETING TIPS

CURRENCY

The official currency in Mallorca, as in the rest of Spain, is the **Euro (€)**, abbreviated as **EUR**. Banknotes are available in denominations of **€5, €10, €20, €50, €100, €200, and €500**, while coins come in values of **1, 2, 5, 10, 20, and 50 cents, as well as €1 and €2 coins**.

The euro is widely used throughout the island, and all businesses, including hotels, restaurants, and shops, accept it as the primary form of payment.

Cash is still commonly used in Mallorca, especially in smaller villages, local markets, and some family-run businesses where credit card payments may not always be accepted. It is advisable to carry some small denominations of euros, particularly for taxis, bus fares, and tips in cafes and restaurants. ATMs (cajeros automáticos) are widely available across the island, particularly in urban centers like Palma and tourist hotspots such as Alcúdia and Magaluf. International visitors can withdraw euros using debit or credit cards, but it is essential to check with your bank regarding **foreign transaction fees** before traveling.

Credit and debit cards, including **Visa, Mastercard, and American Express**, are widely accepted in hotels, restaurants, and larger retail stores. Contactless payments and mobile wallets such as **Apple Pay and Google Pay** are increasingly popular across Mallorca, particularly in urban areas. However, some small businesses, local markets, and rural establishments may only accept cash or have a minimum spend requirement for card payments.

Currency exchange services are available at **airports, banks, and currency exchange offices (casas de cambio)**, though they may charge higher rates and service fees compared to withdrawing cash from an ATM. Banks in Mallorca operate **Monday to Friday from 8:30 AM to 2:00 PM**, with some branches offering limited Saturday morning hours. It is advisable to exchange currency in advance or withdraw cash from ATMs to get better exchange rates.

For those staying in Mallorca for an extended period, opening a **local Spanish bank account** may be beneficial to avoid international transaction fees and simplify financial transactions. Many international and Spanish banks operate branches on the island, including Santander, CaixaBank, and BBVA.

BUDGETING TIPS

Mallorca offers a wide range of options to suit different budgets, from **luxury vacations** to **affordable getaways**. Planning your budget in advance can help maximize your experience while keeping expenses in check.

For **accommodation**, Mallorca has **luxury hotels, boutique stays, budget hostels, and vacation rentals**. If you are looking for an affordable stay, consider **hostels, guesthouses, or Airbnb rentals** outside of Palma's city center. Prices vary by season, with summer (June–August) being the most expensive. Booking accommodation in advance can help secure better deals, especially in spring and autumn when prices are lower, but the weather is still pleasant.

Food expenses can be **high or low**, depending on dining choices. Restaurants in tourist areas tend to be pricier, so opting for **local eateries, tapas bars, and markets** can help save money. Traditional **menú del día (menu of the day)** meals, offered at many Spanish restaurants during lunchtime, provide a full meal (starter, main course, dessert, and drink) for a fixed price, usually between **€10 and €15**. Shopping at **local markets** and grocery stores like Mercadona, Carrefour, or Lidl for fresh produce and preparing your own meals in rental accommodations is another way to cut food costs.

Transportation in Mallorca is **affordable and efficient**. The island has a well-developed public bus system operated by **TIB (Transports de les Illes Balears)** and an affordable train network. A single bus ticket within Palma costs about **€2**, while intercity routes range from **€5 to €10** depending on distance. Renting a car is recommended for exploring rural areas and hidden beaches, but costs can add up with fuel and insurance. To save on car rental, book in advance and compare prices from different providers. Taxis are available but relatively expensive, with fares starting at **€4 and increasing based on distance and time of day**.

For sightseeing, Mallorca offers **many free or low-cost attractions**, such as hiking in the **Serra de Tramuntana**, visiting public beaches, and exploring historic sites like **Alcúdia Old Town**. Museums and cultural sites, including **Palma Cathedral and Bellver Castle**, charge entrance fees ranging from **€5 to €10**, but some offer discounts for students, seniors, and children. Consider purchasing a **Palma Pass** if you plan to visit multiple attractions, as it provides discounts and free public transportation in the city.

Shopping in Mallorca varies from **high-end designer stores** in Palma to **local artisan markets** selling handmade crafts, ceramics, and traditional Mallorcan products like **ensaimadas (pastries), sobrasada (cured sausage), and local wines**. Bargaining is uncommon in fixed-price stores but may be possible in open-air markets.

If you are looking to enjoy nightlife on a budget, many bars offer **happy hour deals** and discounts on cocktails and beer. Entry fees for clubs in areas like **Magaluf and Palma's Paseo Marítimo** can range from **€10 to €30**, depending on the venue and event. Booking club tickets online in advance may help reduce costs.

Mallorca can be enjoyed on a **modest, mid-range, or luxury budget**, and smart spending decisions can help you make the most of your trip without overspending.

VI. LANGUAGE & LOCAL ETIQUETTE

LANGUAGE

The official language of Mallorca is **Spanish (Castellano)**, but the island also has its own regional language, **Catalan**, which is widely spoken and recognized as a co-official language. The local variation of Catalan spoken in Mallorca is called **Mallorquí**, which has distinct pronunciation, vocabulary, and expressions compared to standard Catalan. While Spanish is understood and spoken by nearly all residents, many locals, particularly in rural areas and among older generations, primarily use Mallorquí in daily conversations.

In major tourist areas such as **Palma, Magaluf, and Alcúdia**, English and German are widely spoken due to the high number of international visitors and expatriates. Hotel staff, restaurant workers, and tour operators in these areas are generally proficient in English, making it easy for tourists to communicate. However, in smaller villages and less touristy parts of the island, English may not be as commonly spoken, and basic knowledge of Spanish can be helpful when interacting with locals.

Learning a few basic **Spanish or Mallorquí phrases** can enhance your experience and show respect for the local culture. Here are some useful phrases:

Hola (Spanish) / **Bon dia** (Mallorquí) – Hello

Gracias (Spanish) / **Gràcies** (Mallorquí) – Thank you

Por favor (Spanish) / **Per favor** (Mallorquí) – Please

¿Dónde está...? (Spanish) / **On és...?** (Mallorquí) – Where is...?

La cuenta, por favor (Spanish) / **El compte, per favor** (Mallorquí) – The bill, please

No hablo español (Spanish) / **No parl espanyol** (Mallorquí) – I don't speak Spanish

¿Habla inglés? (Spanish) / **Parla anglès?** (Mallorquí) – Do you speak English?

Although locals in tourist areas are accustomed to communicating in multiple languages, making an effort to speak a few words in Spanish or Mallorquí is greatly appreciated and can lead to a warmer reception.

Mallorca's road signs, public transport announcements, and government documents are often in both **Spanish and Catalan**, so visitors may encounter both languages throughout their stay. While Spanish is more universally understood, recognizing some Catalan words can be useful when navigating the island.

LOCAL ETIQUETTE

Mallorca, like the rest of Spain, has a rich cultural heritage and a laid-back Mediterranean lifestyle. Understanding and respecting local customs and etiquette can help visitors have a more enjoyable and culturally immersive experience.

Greetings and Social Interactions

Mallorcans are generally warm and friendly but may be slightly reserved compared to mainland Spaniards. A common greeting between friends and acquaintances is a **kiss on both cheeks (one on each side)**, while a handshake is more common in formal or business settings. When entering shops or restaurants, it is polite to greet with **"Hola"** or **"Bon dia"** and say **"Gracias"** or **"Adiós"** when leaving.

Dining Etiquette

Eating out is a significant part of Mallorcan culture, and meal times tend to be later than in many other countries. **Lunch (comida)** is typically served between **1:30 PM and 3:30 PM**, and **dinner (cena)** usually starts around **8:30 PM to 10:30 PM**. It is customary to **take**

your time while dining, as meals are seen as social events rather than just eating.

When dining at a restaurant, **waiting for the waiter to bring the bill is expected**, as it is considered impolite to rush customers. To request the check, simply say **"La cuenta, por favor"**. Tipping is not obligatory in Mallorca, but it is appreciated. A tip of **5-10%** in restaurants is common if service was good, while for small cafes and bars, rounding up the bill or leaving a small tip is sufficient.

Dress Code

Mallorca has a relaxed Mediterranean dress code, but certain places require appropriate attire. While **casual beachwear is fine for coastal areas**, wearing swimsuits in towns, restaurants, or public transport is considered disrespectful. Some religious sites, such as **La Seu Cathedral in Palma**, require visitors to **cover their shoulders and knees** before entering.

Respecting Local Culture and Traditions

Mallorca has a strong local identity, and while it is part of Spain, many residents take pride in their **Mallorcan and Catalan heritage**. Being aware of and respecting their culture, language, and traditions is important. Avoid referring to Catalan as a dialect of Spanish, as it is an official and distinct language with deep historical roots.

Many local **festivals and traditions** are celebrated throughout the year, such as **Sant Joan (June 23-24)**, the **Festa de la Beata (September)**, and the **Festa de Sant Antoni (January 16-17)**. These events include processions, bonfires, music, and dancing. Participating in these celebrations is a great way to experience local culture, but it is important to respect customs and traditions.

Environmental Awareness

Mallorca places a strong emphasis on **sustainability and environmental conservation**, particularly due to the high number of tourists visiting the island. Littering is **strictly prohibited**, and many beaches and natural areas have rules against bringing plastic waste or leaving trash behind. In some parts of the island, water conservation is crucial, so visitors are encouraged to **use water responsibly**, especially in rural areas.

Noise and Public Behavior

Mallorcans appreciate a relaxed and peaceful lifestyle, and excessive noise, particularly at night, is frowned upon. While nightlife areas like **Magaluf** are known for partying, it is important to be mindful of **noise levels in residential areas** and avoid disruptive behavior. Public intoxication and rowdy behavior, especially in historic districts and smaller villages, are considered disrespectful.

By following these etiquette guidelines, visitors can enjoy a more authentic and respectful interaction with locals, making their stay in Mallorca a pleasant and memorable experience.

VII. SAFETY & HEALTH GUIDELINES

SAFETY

Mallorca is generally a very safe destination for travelers, with a **low crime rate** and a strong police presence in tourist areas. Violent crime is rare, and the biggest concerns for visitors are **petty theft and scams**, especially in crowded places such as **Palma's Old Town, busy markets, and popular beaches**. Pickpocketing can occur in **tourist hotspots, public transport, and nightlife areas**, so travelers should be cautious with their belongings. It is advisable to keep valuables in a **money belt, crossbody bag, or secure backpack** and avoid carrying large amounts of cash.

Beach safety is another consideration. While Mallorca's beaches are **well-maintained and safe, strong currents** can occur in some areas, especially at **Es Trenc, Cala Mesquida, and Formentor Beach**. Always **pay attention to the colored flag system**, where **red means no swimming, yellow means caution, and green means safe conditions**. Lifeguards are present on most major beaches during peak seasons, but travelers should avoid swimming alone, particularly in secluded areas.

When it comes to road safety, Mallorca's scenic roads, especially in the **Serra de Tramuntana**, can be **narrow and winding**. Drivers should be aware of cyclists, as Mallorca is a popular cycling destination. Speed limits and traffic rules are strictly enforced, and **driving under the influence of alcohol** is severely punished, with roadside checks common. If renting a car, it's recommended to **opt for full insurance coverage** due to the possibility of minor accidents or scratches on narrow streets.

Mallorca has **a safe and reliable public transportation system**, including buses, trains, and taxis. However, when using taxis, it is to **use official taxi stands or book through apps** like **Cabify or Bolt** to avoid overcharging. Unlicensed taxis should be avoided, as they do not operate under regulated pricing and may not be insured.

For nightlife safety, while areas like **Magaluf, Palma's Paseo Marítimo, and El Arenal** are famous for their party scene, travelers should be cautious of **drink spiking and scams** targeting tourists.

It's to **watch your drink, avoid accepting drinks from strangers, and stay in groups** when enjoying the nightlife. Local authorities have cracked down on excessive drunken behavior in certain areas, and **fines can be issued for disorderly conduct in public spaces**.

Regarding natural hazards, **heat exhaustion and dehydration** are concerns during Mallorca's hot summers, where temperatures can exceed **35°C (95°F)**. Travelers should **stay hydrated, use sunscreen, wear hats and light clothing**, and avoid excessive sun exposure, particularly between **12 PM and 4 PM** when the sun is at its strongest.

Emergency services in Mallorca are efficient, and the universal European emergency number **112** can be dialed for police, medical, or fire emergencies. Visitors should also be aware of the **Guardia Civil (national police force)** and the **Policía Local (municipal police)**, who handle different aspects of law enforcement and public safety.

HEALTH GUIDELINES

Mallorca has a high standard of healthcare, with both public and private medical facilities available throughout the island. The public healthcare system (IB-Salut) provides free or low-cost emergency medical care for EU citizens with a valid European Health Insurance Card (EHIC) or Global Health Insurance Card (GHIC) for UK travelers. Non-EU visitors are advised to have travel insurance that covers medical emergencies, as private healthcare costs can be expensive.

There are hospitals and clinics in Palma and other major towns, including Son Espases University Hospital, the largest public hospital on the island. Private hospitals such as Juaneda and Quirónsalud are well-regarded and offer high-quality care, often with English-speaking staff. Pharmacies (farmacias) are widely available and are recognizable by a green cross sign. They are the places to get over-the-counter medication, and many pharmacies have 24-hour emergency service rotations in case of urgent medical needs.

Regarding vaccinations, no specific vaccines are required to enter Mallorca, but it is recommended to be up to date on routine vaccinations, including measles, mumps, rubella (MMR), diphtheria, tetanus, and hepatitis A and B. If visiting from a country with a risk of yellow fever, proof of vaccination may be required.

Mallorca has a strong focus on food safety and hygiene, and it is generally safe to drink tap water, though some visitors prefer bottled water due to the taste of chlorinated tap water. Food poisoning is rare, but travelers should still practice caution when consuming raw seafood or food from street vendors.

For those planning to hike in Mallorca's mountains, it is essential to carry sufficient water, wear proper footwear, and check weather conditions before setting out. In case of hiking accidents, the Mallorca Mountain Rescue Service is available for assistance. Heatstroke and dehydration are common concerns, so travelers should take breaks and avoid strenuous activities during peak heat hours.

If travelers require prescription medication, they should bring enough supply for the trip and carry a copy of their doctor's prescription in case customs officials request it. Most common medications are available in Mallorca's pharmacies, but brand names may differ from those in other countries.

Mallorca provides a safe and healthy environment for travelers, but following basic health precautions and understanding local healthcare options ensures a stress-free and enjoyable visit.

CHAPTER 1: SOME ATTRACTIONS & MUST-SEE LANDMARKS

I. PALMA CATHEDRAL (LA SEU)

Address: Carrer del Mirador, 07001 Palma, Illes Balears, Spain

P alma Cathedral, commonly known as **La Seu**, is one of Mallorca's most iconic landmarks and a masterpiece of **Gothic architecture**. Located in the heart of Palma de Mallorca, overlooking the **Bay of Palma**, this stunning cathedral is a symbol of the island's rich history, religious significance, and architectural brilliance.

The construction of La Seu began in **1229**, commissioned by **King James I of Aragon** after his conquest of Mallorca from the Moors. It was built on the site of a former **Moorish mosque**, reflecting the island's transition from Islamic to Christian rule. However, the cathedral was not completed until **1601**, with various additions and modifications made over the centuries.

One of the most striking features of La Seu is its **grand façade**, adorned with intricate stone carvings, pointed arches, and massive flying buttresses. The main entrance, known as the **Portal del Mirador**, faces the sea and features elaborate Gothic sculptures. The **South Wall**, which runs along Parc de la Mar, is one of the most photographed parts of the cathedral due to its imposing height and dramatic architectural elements.

The cathedral's **interior** is equally breathtaking, with a **nave that soars up to 44 meters (144 feet)**, making it one of the tallest Gothic structures in Europe. The **central nave** is flanked by enormous columns and filled with stained glass windows that bathe the space in colorful light. The most famous of these is the **Great Rose Window**, measuring nearly **14 meters (46 feet) in diameter** and consisting of over **1,200 pieces of stained glass**. When sunlight passes through this window, the effect is mesmerizing, creating a kaleidoscope of colors on the stone walls.

One of the most notable renovations of La Seu was led by **Antoni Gaudí**, the famous Catalan architect, in the early 20th century. Gaudí introduced modernist elements, including a suspended **candelabrum over the altar**, improved lighting, and a reconfiguration of the choir stalls to open up the interior space. His influence, though subtle compared to his works in Barcelona, added a unique artistic touch to the cathedral.

Another remarkable feature inside the cathedral is the **Chapel of the Holy Sacrament**, redesigned by contemporary artist **Miquel Barceló** in 2007. The chapel's walls are covered in a **ceramic mural depicting biblical scenes**, blending traditional religious themes with a modern artistic approach.

The cathedral complex also includes a **museum**, where visitors can view religious artifacts, paintings, sculptures, and historical documents related to La Seu's history.

Due to its historical and architectural significance, La Seu remains one of the most visited attractions in Mallorca. It is also an active place of worship, hosting **regular Mass services, religious ceremonies, and special events**, including Easter and Christmas celebrations.

Visitors can explore La Seu both inside and out, with **guided tours available** for those who want to learn more about its history, construction, and artistic elements. The cathedral is located in

Palma's historic center, making it easily accessible from other major attractions such as **Almudaina Palace, Parc de la Mar, and Palma's Old Town**.

With its **stunning Gothic architecture, vibrant stained glass, and rich historical background**, La Seu is a must-visit for anyone traveling to Mallorca. Whether you are interested in history, architecture, or spirituality, the cathedral offers a truly unforgettable experience.

II. SERRA DE TRAMUNTANA

Address: Serra de Tramuntana, 07109 Fornalutx, Illes Balears, Spain

The **Serra de Tramuntana** is a breathtaking mountain range that stretches along the **northwest coast of Mallorca**, covering approximately **90 kilometers (56 miles)** from **Andratx in the southwest to Cap de Formentor in the northeast**. It is the island's most significant natural landscape, known for its **dramatic cliffs, rugged peaks, picturesque villages, and terraced olive groves**. The mountain range was designated a **UNESCO World Heritage Site in 2011** due to its cultural and environmental importance.

The highest peak in the range is **Puig Major**, standing at **1,436 meters (4,711 feet)**, making it the tallest mountain in the **Balearic Islands**. Due to its strategic importance, the peak itself is a restricted military zone, but nearby summits like **Puig de Massanella (1,364 meters)** offer stunning panoramic views and are accessible to hikers.

The **Serra de Tramuntana** is famous for its **charming mountain villages**, each offering a unique glimpse into traditional Mallorcan life. **Valldemossa**, known for its **Cartoixa de Valldemossa monastery**, was once home to **composer Frédéric Chopin and writer George Sand**, who spent a winter here in 1838. **Deià**, a scenic coastal village, has long been a retreat for artists, musicians, and writers, including **poet Robert Graves. Sóller**, nestled in a lush valley of orange groves, is known for its historic **wooden train** that connects it to Palma and its picturesque **Port de Sóller**. Other notable towns include **Fornalutx**, often called the "prettiest village in Spain," and **Banyalbufar**, known for its terraced vineyards and breathtaking sea views.

One of the most famous attractions within the **Serra de Tramuntana** is the **Sa Calobra Road**, a twisting mountain road with

hairpin turns that leads to **Torrent de Pareis**, a spectacular gorge where towering cliffs form a dramatic natural amphitheater. The drive itself is a highlight for visitors, offering stunning views and a thrilling experience for motorists and cyclists.

The mountain range is a paradise for **outdoor enthusiasts**, particularly **hikers and cyclists**. The **Dry Stone Route (GR-221)** is a well-known **long-distance hiking trail** that runs through the Serra de Tramuntana, covering ancient stone pathways that connect remote villages, forests, and breathtaking viewpoints. Shorter trails lead to hidden coves, like **Cala Tuent**, or historical sites, such as the **Torre del Verger**, an old watchtower with panoramic views of the coastline.

Cycling is also extremely popular in the **Serra de Tramuntana**, with professional and amateur cyclists tackling the steep mountain roads. The **climb to Sa Calobra, the Coll de Sóller, and the route to Cap de Formentor** are some of the most famous cycling routes in Europe.

Agriculture has played a vital role in shaping the landscape of the **Serra de Tramuntana**, with ancient **olive groves, almond**

orchards, and vineyards thriving on the steep terraces. The traditional dry-stone walling technique used to build terraces and paths is part of the region's cultural heritage. Visitors can explore historic **fincas (rural estates)**, many of which have been converted into **boutique hotels, agrotourism lodges, or local farms producing olive oil and wine**.

The **Serra de Tramuntana** also has rich **wildlife and biodiversity**, with **rare birds, wild goats, and diverse Mediterranean flora**. Birdwatchers can spot species such as **black vultures, peregrine falcons, and Eleonora's falcons**, particularly around the remote cliffs of **Cap de Formentor**.

In addition to its natural beauty, the region is home to **important cultural and historical sites**, including ancient monasteries, churches, and Moorish-built irrigation systems. The **Sanctuary of Lluc**, a religious and pilgrimage site, houses the famous **Black Madonna statue** and is a spiritual center in Mallorca.

Visiting the **Serra de Tramuntana** offers a blend of **nature, culture, and adventure**, making it a must-see destination for anyone exploring Mallorca. Whether driving along scenic mountain roads, hiking through olive groves, cycling challenging routes, or simply enjoying the peaceful atmosphere of a village café, the **Serra de Tramuntana** provides an unforgettable experience of Mallorca's wild and unspoiled beauty.

III. CUEVAS DEL DRACH (DRAGON CAVES)

Address: Ctra. de les Coves, s/n, 07680 Porto Cristo, Illes Balears, Spain

The **Cuevas del Drach (Dragon Caves)** are one of the most spectacular natural wonders in Mallorca, located in **Porto Cristo**, on the island's east coast. These stunning limestone caves extend for approximately **1,200 meters (3,940 feet)** and reach depths of **up to 25 meters (82 feet)** below ground level. The caves are famous for their **dramatic stalactites and stalagmites**, unique rock formations, and the breathtaking **underground lake, Lago Martel**, one of the largest subterranean lakes in the world.

The formation of the **Cuevas del Drach** dates back **millions of years**, shaped by water erosion and geological activity. They were first mentioned in historical records in the **14th century**, but it wasn't until the **19th century** that French geologist **Édouard-Alfred**

Martel conducted an extensive exploration, discovering the large underground lake that now bears his name. Today, the caves are one of Mallorca's most visited attractions, drawing thousands of tourists each year.

The interior of the **Cuevas del Drach** is divided into four main caves:

Cueva Negra (Black Cave)

Cueva Blanca (White Cave)

Cueva de Luis Salvador (Luis Salvador Cave)

Cueva de los Franceses (Cave of the French)

Each section features an otherworldly landscape of **towering stalactites, eerie rock formations, and shimmering pools of water**. Artificial lighting has been carefully installed to highlight the caves' natural beauty while maintaining a mystical ambiance.

One of the highlights of visiting the **Cuevas del Drach** is the **live classical music concert** held inside the caves. This unique experience takes place near **Lago Martel**, where musicians perform pieces by **Chopin, Schubert, and other classical composers** while floating on illuminated boats. The acoustics within the caves create a mesmerizing atmosphere, making this a truly unforgettable moment for visitors.

After the concert, guests are given the option to **take a short boat ride across Lago Martel**, experiencing the peacefulness of the underground lake while surrounded by breathtaking rock formations. Alternatively, visitors can walk along a bridge that crosses the lake.

The temperature inside the caves remains at a **constant 18-21°C (64-70°F)**, making it a comfortable experience year-round. The guided tour lasts approximately **one hour** and covers **about 1.2 kilometers (0.75 miles)** of well-maintained pathways. Due to the caves' natural terrain, the tour includes stairs, so it may not be fully accessible for individuals with mobility challenges.

Outside the caves, the site features **a gift shop, café, and landscaped gardens**, making it a great spot to relax after the tour. Porto Cristo itself is a charming coastal town, known for its **beautiful marina, sandy beaches, and seafood restaurants**, making it a good place to explore before or after visiting the caves.

The **Cuevas del Drach** are open **year-round**, with tours available in multiple languages, including **Spanish, English, German, and French**. Tickets can be purchased online or at the entrance, but it is recommended to book in advance, especially during peak tourist seasons, as the tours can sell out quickly.

Whether you are a nature lover, history enthusiast, or simply looking for a unique experience in Mallorca, the **Cuevas del Drach** offer a **magical underground adventure** unlike any other. The combination of stunning rock formations, a serene underground lake, and an enchanting classical music concert makes this an absolute must-visit attraction on the island.

IV. CAP DE FORMENTOR

Address: Cap de Formentor, 07460 Pollença, Illes Balears, Spain

Cap de Formentor is one of the most breathtaking natural landmarks in Mallorca, located at the **northernmost point of the island** on the **Formentor Peninsula**. Known for its **dramatic cliffs, stunning panoramic views, winding roads, and crystal-clear**

waters, this rugged cape is a must-visit destination for nature lovers, photographers, and adventure seekers.

The **journey to Cap de Formentor** is an experience in itself. The road leading to the cape, the **Ma-2210**, is a scenic but challenging drive, featuring **hairpin turns, steep inclines, and narrow passages**. Designed by the famous Italian engineer **Antonio Parietti**, the same architect responsible for the **Sa Calobra Road**, this winding route offers spectacular views at every turn. Many visitors choose to **cycle or hike** along parts of the road, as it provides an exhilarating experience with stunning coastal landscapes. The route passes through dense pine forests and rocky cliffs, with **several scenic viewpoints (miradors)** along the way.

One of the most famous stops before reaching the cape is the **Mirador Es Colomer**, a spectacular viewpoint offering breathtaking views over the rugged coastline and deep-blue Mediterranean Sea. This spot is named after **Illa del Colomer**, a small rocky island visible from the viewpoint. **Sunset and sunrise** are particularly magical at this location, as the golden light enhances the beauty of the cliffs and sea.

Further along the road, visitors will come across **Formentor Beach (Platja de Formentor)**, a picturesque white-sand beach with **turquoise waters and lush pine trees** providing shade. This beach is known for its **calm, clear waters**, making it for swimming, kayaking, and snorkeling. It is also home to the historic **Formentor Hotel**, which has hosted famous guests like **Winston Churchill, Charlie Chaplin, and Audrey Hepburn**.

At the very end of the peninsula stands the iconic **Formentor Lighthouse (Far de Formentor)**, one of the most remote and spectacular lighthouses in Spain. Perched atop a **210-meter (689-foot) high cliff**, the lighthouse was built in **1863** and has guided sailors through the **Balearic Sea** for over a century. The lighthouse area provides **unparalleled panoramic views** of the sea and cliffs, stretching as far as **Menorca on clear days**. The wind and crashing waves create a wild, untamed atmosphere, making it one of the most **dramatic and awe-inspiring locations** on the island.

Due to its **popularity and environmental concerns, Cap de Formentor is closed to private vehicles during peak summer months (June to September)**, typically from **10 AM to 7 PM**. During this time, visitors must use **shuttle buses from Port de Pollença** or cycle/walk to the cape. This restriction helps preserve the fragile ecosystem and reduces congestion on the narrow roads.

The **wildlife and flora** of Cap de Formentor are also noteworthy. The cliffs are home to **rare birds**, including **Eleonora's falcons, peregrine falcons, and ospreys**, making it an excellent location for birdwatching. The rocky terrain is covered with **Mediterranean vegetation, including wild rosemary, juniper, and olive trees**, creating a unique and unspoiled landscape.

Cap de Formentor is an **absolute must-visit** for those exploring Mallorca, offering a combination of **adventure, natural beauty, and unforgettable views**. Whether you choose to **drive, hike, cycle, or take a shuttle**, the journey to this remote and rugged cape will undoubtedly be one of the most memorable experiences on the island.

V. BELLVER CASTLE

Address: Carrer de Camilo José Cela, s/n, 07014 Palma, Illes Balears, Spain

Bellver Castle (Castell de Bellver) is a stunning **14th-century Gothic-style fortress** located on a **hilltop overlooking Palma de**

Mallorca. It is one of the most unique castles in Spain due to its **circular design**, a rare feature among European medieval castles. Positioned **112 meters (367 feet) above sea level**, the castle offers **spectacular panoramic views** of **Palma Bay, the Serra de Tramuntana mountains, and the surrounding countryside**.

The castle was **commissioned by King James II of Mallorca in 1300** as a **royal residence**. Its circular structure, inspired by Roman and Eastern Mediterranean fortresses, consists of a **central courtyard surrounded by a two-story colonnade**, four large towers, and a **12-meter-high moat**. The main entrance is connected to the castle by a **stone bridge** leading to the impressive **gothic doorway**.

Bellver Castle has had a long and varied history, serving as a **royal palace, military stronghold, and prison** over the centuries. It housed **Mallorcan monarchs**, including **King James III's widow and children** after the kingdom of Mallorca was incorporated into the Crown of Aragon. Later, it was used as a **military prison**, holding notable figures such as **Gaspar Melchor de Jovellanos, a Spanish writer and politician,** during the Napoleonic Wars. It continued to function as a prison until the 20th century.

Today, Bellver Castle is **one of Palma's most visited cultural landmarks** and houses the **City History Museum (Museu d'Història de la Ciutat)**, which showcases artifacts, models, and exhibits detailing **Palma's history from Roman times to the modern era**. The museum provides insights into the city's development, maritime trade, and the castle's own historical significance.

The **castle's interior** is an architectural marvel, featuring **Gothic ribbed vaults, large arched windows, and an open courtyard** that once hosted royal ceremonies and events. The upper level, accessible via a **spiral staircase**, offers breathtaking **360-degree views** of Palma and the Mediterranean. Visitors can explore **the chapel, dungeons, watchtower, and storerooms**, which provide a glimpse into the castle's medieval past.

Surrounding the castle is **Bellver Forest (Bosque de Bellver)**, a lush pine forest that serves as **a natural park with walking trails, picnic areas, and viewpoints**. It is a popular spot for both tourists and locals, offering a peaceful escape from the city.

Bellver Castle is open to the public year-round, with **guided tours available in multiple languages**. Many visitors recommend **coming in the late afternoon or early evening** to witness the stunning sunset views over Palma. The castle also hosts **concerts, cultural events, and historical reenactments**, making it a dynamic attraction beyond its historical significance.

Whether for its **fascinating history, unique architecture, or breathtaking views**, **Bellver Castle** is a must-visit destination in Mallorca.

CHAPTER 2: RECOMMENDED BEACHES & COASTAL SPOTS

I. PLAYA DE MURO

Address: Playa de Muro, 07458 Muro, Illes Balears, Spain

Playa de Muro is one of Mallorca's most stunning and family-friendly beaches, stretching over 6 kilometers (3.7 miles) along the northeastern coast of the island, near Alcúdia. Known for its fine white sand, shallow turquoise waters, and modern beach facilities, it is a top destination for both relaxation and water activities. As part of the Bay of Alcúdia, it is one of the longest beaches in Mallorca and is divided into several sections, each offering a slightly different atmosphere.

The beach is characterized by soft, powdery sand and crystal-clear, shallow waters, making it an ideal location for families with children. The shallow depth extends far out into the sea, allowing for safe swimming and wading. The gentle waves and warm water temperatures, particularly during the summer months, make Playa de Muro for relaxing swims, paddleboarding, and floating.

One of the most notable features of Playa de Muro is its well-maintained facilities, including sunbeds, umbrellas, showers, and lifeguard services. Along the beach, visitors will find beach bars (chiringuitos), restaurants, and resorts, offering most things from casual snacks to fine dining with beachfront views. The presence of luxury hotels and family-friendly resorts in the area makes Playa de Muro a convenient and comfortable beach destination.

For those looking for adventure and water sports, Playa de Muro offers a wide range of activities, including jet skiing, windsurfing, kitesurfing, and stand-up paddleboarding. There are also opportunities for boat trips and snorkeling excursions to nearby spots like Formentor Peninsula and Alcúdia Bay. The wooden pier located on the beach is a popular spot for photographs, offering a picturesque view of the turquoise waters.

The beach is divided into different sections:

Sector 1: The busiest and most developed area, featuring luxury hotels, restaurants, and bars.

Sector 2: A quieter stretch with a more natural setting and fewer facilities.

Es Comú de Muro: A protected nature reserve with dunes and pine forests, offering a more secluded and unspoiled atmosphere.

Es Capellans: A small section near Can Picafort, with a laid-back vibe and traditional beach bars.

Another highlight of Playa de Muro is its proximity to S'Albufera Natural Park, the largest wetland area in the Balearic Islands. This park is a haven for birdwatchers and nature lovers, home to over 200 species of birds, as well as diverse plant life and scenic walking trails. Many visitors combine a trip to the beach with a visit to this beautiful nature reserve.

Playa de Muro is also a great location for sunset views, with the sky turning shades of orange and pink over the calm waters. The area comes alive in the evenings, with beachfront bars and restaurants offering cocktails, live music, and Mediterranean cuisine.

With its combination of natural beauty, excellent amenities, and a variety of activities, Playa de Muro is a must-visit beach in Mallorca. Whether you're looking for family-friendly relaxation, thrilling water sports, or a peaceful escape into nature, this beach offers something for every type of traveler.

II. CALA AGULLA

Address: Cala Agulla, 07590 Capdepera, Illes Balears, Spain

Cala Agulla is one of the most beautiful and **unspoiled beaches** in Mallorca, located on the **northeastern coast** of the island, near the town of **Cala Ratjada** and the municipality of **Capdepera**. This stunning beach is renowned for its **soft golden sand, crystal-clear turquoise waters, and natural surroundings**, making it a favorite destination for both locals and tourists seeking a **relaxing and scenic beach experience**.

Measuring approximately 500 meters (1,640 feet) in length and 50 meters (164 feet) in width, Cala Agulla offers plenty of space for visitors to sunbathe, swim, and enjoy the pristine environment. The beach is **surrounded by lush pine forests, dunes, and rocky cliffs**, which contribute to its **protected status as a Natural Area of Special Interest (ANEI)**. Because of this status, Cala Agulla has been carefully preserved, with **limited commercial development** to maintain its natural beauty.

The **waters at Cala Agulla are exceptionally clear**, with gentle waves and a shallow shoreline, making it an ideal beach for **families with children, swimmers, and snorkeling enthusiasts**. The **soft sandy seabed** and gradually deepening waters create conditions for both relaxation and water activities. The beach has been awarded the **Blue Flag**, a certification that recognizes high environmental and water quality standards.

For **water sports lovers**, Cala Agulla offers various activities, including **paddleboarding, kayaking, jet skiing, and snorkeling**. The surrounding rocky coves are excellent spots for **snorkeling and exploring marine life**, while the open waters further from the shore provide an exciting playground for those seeking a more adventurous experience.

Facilities and services at Cala Agulla include:

Sunbed and umbrella rentals

Lifeguard service for safety

Beachside bars and restaurants (offering snacks, drinks, and traditional Mediterranean cuisine)

Public restrooms and showers

Water sports equipment rentals

Although Cala Agulla is not as heavily developed as some other tourist beaches in Mallorca, its proximity to the lively town of **Cala Ratjada** means visitors have easy access to **hotels, restaurants, bars, and shops** just a short drive or walk away. The town is known for its **vibrant nightlife**, making it a great option for those looking to combine a beach day with evening entertainment.

Hiking and nature lovers will also find plenty to explore around Cala Agulla. Several **hiking trails** lead from the beach to other nearby natural spots, such as **Cala Mesquida** and the **Llevant Peninsula Natural Park**, offering stunning coastal views and opportunities to spot local wildlife.

One of the most magical aspects of Cala Agulla is its **sunset views**. As the sun sets over the hills and forests behind the beach, the sky transforms into beautiful hues of pink and orange, making it a **spot for evening relaxation and photography**.

While Cala Agulla is a **popular destination**, it is busiest during the **summer months (June to September)**. To avoid crowds, it is recommended to visit **early in the morning or later in the afternoon**. Additionally, parking near the beach is available but can fill up quickly, so arriving early ensures a more hassle-free experience.

Thanks to its **pristine natural beauty, excellent swimming conditions, and family-friendly atmosphere**, Cala Agulla is one of **Mallorca's must-visit beaches**. Whether you want to unwind on the soft sand, explore the underwater world, or take in the breathtaking coastal scenery, Cala Agulla offers an unforgettable beach experience in one of the most picturesque settings on the island.

III. ES TRENC

Address: Es Trenc Beach, 07639 Campos, Illes Balears, Spain

Es Trenc is one of Mallorca's most famous and unspoiled beaches, located on the south coast of the island, near the town of Campos. This pristine, 2-kilometer-long stretch of soft white sand and crystal-clear turquoise waters is often compared to the Caribbean, thanks to its stunning colors and lack of heavy development. Es Trenc is part of a protected natural reserve, meaning it has remained free from large resorts and urbanization, preserving its wild and natural beauty.

The waters at Es Trenc are shallow, warm, and incredibly clear, making it an ideal destination for swimming, sunbathing, and relaxing. The beach is family-friendly due to the gradual depth of the sea, but it is also popular with couples, solo travelers, and nature lovers looking for a peaceful retreat. The sand is fine and powdery, for barefoot walks along the shoreline.

One of the unique aspects of Es Trenc is its natural surroundings. Behind the beach, you'll find dunes, pine trees, and salt flats, which are home to diverse wildlife, including migratory birds like flamingos. The nearby Salinas d'Es Trenc is a famous salt production area, where traditional Mallorcan sea salt (Flor de Sal d'Es Trenc) is harvested.

While Es Trenc is protected from overdevelopment, it does have basic amenities, including:

Sunbeds and umbrellas for rent

A few beach bars (chiringuitos) offering drinks, snacks, and fresh seafood

Public restrooms and showers

Lifeguards on duty during peak hours

Es Trenc is also one of Mallorca's most popular nudist-friendly beaches, with certain sections designated for naturists. However, clothing is optional, and the beach welcomes all types of visitors.

Because of its beauty and protected status, Es Trenc can get crowded during peak summer months (June to August). The favourable time to visit is early in the morning or later in the afternoon, when it is less busy, and the light is for photography.

Getting to Es Trenc requires some planning, as there are no direct public transport options. Visitors must drive or take a taxi, and there is a paid parking lot nearby, though spaces fill up quickly in the summer. The beach is about 10 km from Campos and 45 km from Palma.

Es Trenc is ideal for those seeking a natural, tranquil, and scenic beach experience. Whether you want to swim in its crystal-clear waters, explore the salt flats, or simply relax in a preserved Mediterranean paradise, Es Trenc offers a true escape from the crowds and commercialization of Mallorca's resort areas.

IV. CALA MONDRAGÓ

Address: Cala Mondragó, 07691 Santanyí, Illes Balears, Spain

Cala Mondragó is one of Mallorca's most picturesque and unspoiled beaches, located on the southeastern coast near Santanyí. It lies within the Mondragó Natural Park, a protected nature reserve known for its diverse wildlife, lush pine forests, rocky cliffs, and scenic coastal trails. Due to its pristine beauty, crystal-clear turquoise waters, and soft white sand, Cala Mondragó is often ranked among the beaches in Mallorca.

The beach is relatively small, about 75 meters (246 feet) wide, creating an intimate and peaceful atmosphere. The shallow, calm waters make it an ideal spot for families with children, while the rocky coves and underwater marine life attract snorkelers and nature lovers. The seabed is mostly sandy with patches of seagrass, making it a location for snorkeling and swimming in the warm Mediterranean waters.

Cala Mondragó is part of a protected area, meaning there are no large hotels or commercial developments nearby, which has helped preserve its natural charm. However, visitors can find basic amenities, including:

Lifeguard service during peak hours

Sunbeds and umbrellas for rent

Public restrooms and showers

A small beachside bar (chiringuito) offering drinks and snacks

Nearby restaurants and picnic areas within the natural park

A highlight of visiting Cala Mondragó is the opportunity to explore the Mondragó Natural Park, which offers several hiking and cycling trails. The coastal paths provide breathtaking views of the rugged cliffs, coves, and the Mediterranean Sea, making it an excellent area for nature walks. The park is home to various bird species, wildflowers, and unique Mediterranean vegetation, making it a paradise for birdwatchers and wildlife enthusiasts.

Nearby, visitors can also access Cala S'Amarador, a slightly larger but equally beautiful beach located just a short walk away. The two beaches are connected by a scenic coastal path, offering an easy and enjoyable way to explore both areas.

Because of its natural beauty and accessibility, Cala Mondragó can get crowded during the peak summer months (June to August). To fully enjoy the peaceful surroundings, it is to arrive early in the morning or visit during the off-season (spring and autumn), when the park is quieter.

Getting to Cala Mondragó is relatively easy. It is located about 10 km from Santanyí and 65 km from Palma. Visitors can reach the beach by car, bicycle, or public transport. There is a paid parking lot nearby, from which it's a short walk to the beach. During the summer, local buses from Cala d'Or and Santanyí also provide direct access.

Cala Mondragó is a good beach for those looking to experience Mallorca's natural beauty, clear waters, and a tranquil environment. Whether you want to swim, snorkel, hike, or simply relax on the soft sand, this beach offers a true Mediterranean paradise within a protected nature reserve.

V. SA CALOBRA

Address: Sa Calobra, 07315 Escorca, Illes Balears, Spain

Sa Calobra is one of the most breathtaking and unique destinations in Mallorca, located on the **northwestern coast** within the **Serra de Tramuntana**, a UNESCO World Heritage Site. Known for its **dramatic cliffs, crystal-clear waters, and the famous Torrent de Pareis gorge**, Sa Calobra offers a combination of **natural beauty, adventure, and a secluded beach experience** that attracts visitors from all over the world.

Getting to Sa Calobra is an **adventure in itself**. The road leading to this remote cove, the **MA-2141**, is considered one of the most scenic and challenging drives in Europe. Designed by the Italian engineer **Antonio Parietti** in the 1930s, the road features **12 kilometers (7.5 miles) of winding turns, steep descents, and breathtaking views**. One of the most famous sections of the road is the **Nus de Sa Corbata (Tie Knot Bend)**, a **270-degree hairpin turn** that loops around itself, offering an exhilarating driving or cycling experience. Because of its dramatic curves and stunning scenery, the road is popular among **cyclists, motorcyclists, and driving enthusiasts**.

For those who prefer a **more relaxed journey**, Sa Calobra is also accessible by **boat from Port de Sóller**. The boat trip offers a scenic ride along Mallorca's **rugged coastline**, providing spectacular views of **hidden coves, towering cliffs, and the open Mediterranean Sea** before arriving at the picturesque bay of Sa Calobra.

Once at Sa Calobra, visitors are greeted by a **small pebble beach with turquoise waters**, nestled between towering cliffs. The **crystal-clear sea** makes it an ideal spot for **swimming and snorkeling**, with **rocky formations and marine life** creating a beautiful underwater landscape. Despite its remote location, Sa Calobra has a few **basic amenities**, including **restaurants, cafes, and restrooms**, but it remains largely untouched by commercial development.

A **short walk through a tunnel carved into the cliffs** leads to the **Torrent de Pareis**, one of Mallorca's most spectacular natural wonders. This **dramatic gorge**, formed by millions of years of water erosion, features **towering canyon walls reaching up to 200 meters (656 feet) high**, with a dried riverbed that fills with water after heavy rains. During the **summer months**, the gorge provides an unforgettable hiking experience, allowing visitors to explore the rugged terrain and unique rock formations.

The **Torrent de Pareis hike** is one of the most **challenging and rewarding hikes** in Mallorca. Starting from **Escorca**, this 3-4 hour trek follows the **riverbed through caves, boulders, and narrow passages**, eventually opening up to the stunning beach at Sa Calobra. The hike is suited for **experienced hikers**, as it requires **climbing, scrambling, and navigating uneven terrain**, especially after heavy rains when parts of the gorge may be flooded.

Due to its **remote location and natural beauty**, Sa Calobra can become **crowded during peak tourist season (June to September)**. To enjoy a more peaceful experience, it is recommended to **arrive early in the morning or visit during the off-season (spring or autumn)** when the area is quieter.

Sa Calobra remains one of Mallorca's **must-visit locations**, offering a unique blend of **adventure, dramatic landscapes, and crystal-clear waters**. Whether you **drive along the winding road, take a boat trip, hike through the Torrent de Pareis, or simply relax on the secluded beach**, a visit to Sa Calobra is an **unforgettable experience** in one of the most stunning parts of the island.

CHAPTER 3: OUTDOOR ADVENTURES & ACTIVITIES

I. HIKING IN TRAMUNTANA

Address: Serra de Tramuntana, 07109 Fornalutx, Illes Balears, Spain

Hiking in the Serra de Tramuntana is one of the most rewarding outdoor experiences in Mallorca, offering a mix of rugged mountain landscapes, coastal views, ancient paths, and charming villages. This UNESCO World Heritage Site stretches along the northwestern coast of the island, covering nearly 90 kilometers (56 miles) and providing diverse trails for all levels of hikers.

The terrain of the Tramuntana mountains varies from forested valleys and limestone cliffs to dry-stone terraces and panoramic summits. Many of the trails follow ancient routes used by shepherds, traders, and pilgrims, adding a historical dimension to the hikes. The favourable time for hiking is during the cooler months, from October to May, as summer temperatures can be extreme, making some routes challenging in the heat.

One of the most popular long-distance routes is the GR-221, also known as the Dry Stone Route (Ruta de Pedra en Sec). This classic 8-stage trail runs from Port d'Andratx to Pollença, passing through Valldemossa, Deià, Sóller, and Lluc Monastery. The full route is about 140 kilometers (87 miles) and takes several days to complete, but many hikers choose to do shorter sections as day hikes.

For those looking for shorter hikes, there are several options:

The Archduke's Trail (Camí de s'Arxiduc): Starting from Valldemossa, this moderate-to-challenging hike follows a high ridge with breathtaking coastal and mountain views. It was created by Archduke Ludwig Salvator of Austria in the 19th century and remains one of the most scenic routes in Mallorca.

Barranc de Biniaraix: Beginning in Sóller, this historic stone-paved path winds through gorges, olive groves, and waterfalls, offering a peaceful yet steep ascent toward L'Ofre Peak (1,093 meters).

Deià to Sóller Coastal Walk: A relatively easy and scenic hike that follows the coastline, passing through rocky cliffs, pine forests, and hidden coves. This route connects the artistic village of Deià with the charming town of Sóller.

Tossals Verds: A circular route near Lluc and Cúber Reservoir, featuring rocky trails, caves, and impressive mountain views. This moderate hike is a favorite among nature lovers and experienced trekkers.

For advanced hikers, Puig de Massanella (1,364 meters) is the second-highest accessible peak in Mallorca and offers panoramic views of the island and the Mediterranean Sea. The trail is challenging, with steep ascents and rocky terrain, but it is one of the most rewarding climbs in the Tramuntana range.

Hiking in the Tramuntana offers diverse wildlife and flora, including wild goats, falcons, ancient olive trees, and Mediterranean pine forests. Some trails also pass historic sites, such as Moorish-built irrigation systems, medieval watchtowers, and monasteries like Lluc Sanctuary, a famous pilgrimage site.

Important hiking tips:

Always carry enough water, especially in summer.

Wear proper hiking shoes, as some trails have uneven and rocky terrain.

Check the weather forecast, as fog, rain, and strong winds can make certain trails dangerous.

Some routes require permits or entrance fees, especially around private estates.

If hiking alone, inform someone about your route, as some areas have limited mobile phone signal.

The Serra de Tramuntana is a paradise for hikers, offering most things from easy walks through olive groves to demanding mountain ascents. Whether you are looking for a relaxing nature walk, a multi-day trekking adventure, or a challenging summit climb, hiking in this stunning mountain range provides an unforgettable experience in Mallorca.

II. WATERSPORTS & DIVING

El Toro Marine Reserve (Diving & Snorkeling)
Address: Scuba Activa, Carrer d'Es Traves, 21, 07108 Port de Sóller, Illes Balears, Spain

El Toro Marine Reserve, located on the southwest coast of Mallorca, is one of the island's most spectacular diving and snorkeling destinations. Established as a protected marine reserve in 2004, it has become a haven for marine biodiversity, offering some of the clearest waters and richest underwater ecosystems in the Balearic Islands. The reserve is situated near El Toro Island, a small rocky islet off the coast of Santa Ponsa, and is easily accessible from Palma, Magaluf, and Port Adriano.

Due to its protected status, fishing is strictly prohibited, allowing marine life to thrive. The waters around El Toro are teeming with fish and coral, making it a top spot for scuba divers and snorkelers. Divers can expect to see groupers, barracudas, moray eels, octopuses, stingrays, and even occasional dolphins or sunfish (Mola mola). The underwater landscape features a mix of rocky reefs, caves, and sandy bottoms, offering diverse diving experiences.

There are multiple dive sites in the El Toro Marine Reserve, catering to different skill levels:

El Toro Reef: One of the most famous sites, with massive schools of fish and stunning rock formations.

El Toro Caves: For more advanced divers, these underwater caves offer an exciting challenge.

El Toro Plateau: Ideal for beginners, with shallower depths and vibrant marine life.

The visibility in the water is excellent, often reaching up to 30 meters (98 feet), making it for both scuba diving and snorkeling. While divers can explore deeper sections (up to 40 meters/131 feet), snorkelers can stay closer to the surface, where they can still observe a variety of fish and coral formations.

El Toro is a must-visit for underwater enthusiasts, with diving centers in nearby Santa Ponsa, Magaluf, and Palmanova offering guided tours, equipment rentals, and certification courses. The favourable time to dive here is from May to October, when water temperatures are warmer and visibility is at its .

Whether you're a certified diver looking for an unforgettable experience or a snorkeler wanting to explore Mallorca's marine life, El Toro Marine Reserve is one of the top aquatic destinations on the island. Its protected status, rich biodiversity, and stunning underwater landscapes make it a paradise for anyone passionate about the ocean.

Playa de Palma (Jet Skiing & Parasailing)
Address: Water Sports Mallorca, Avinguda de Fra Joan Llabrés, 9, 07600 Palma, Illes Balears, Spain

Playa de Palma is one of Mallorca's most vibrant and action-packed beaches, stretching over **6 kilometers (3.7 miles)** along the **southeast coast** of the island, just **10 km from Palma city center**. This beach is well known for its **soft golden sand, clear blue waters, and lively atmosphere**, making it a top destination for **jet skiing, parasailing, and other watersports**.

One of the biggest attractions at Playa de Palma is **jet skiing**, an adrenaline-pumping activity that lets riders speed across the **crystal-clear Mediterranean waters** while enjoying spectacular views of the **beachfront, palm-lined promenades, and distant mountains**. Jet ski rentals and guided tours are widely available along the beach, with options for both **beginners and experienced riders**. Most jet ski excursions include **safety briefings, life jackets, and guided routes**, allowing visitors to explore scenic coastlines, hidden coves, and even nearby islets.

Parasailing at Playa de Palma offers an entirely different but equally thrilling experience. Participants are strapped into a **parachute and lifted high above the sea**, where they can enjoy **panoramic aerial views of the coastline, turquoise waters, and the stunning Palma Bay**. Flights typically reach heights of **50 to 100 meters (164 to 328 feet)**, providing a unique perspective of the island's beauty. Many parasailing providers offer **solo, tandem, or triple flights**, making it a great activity for individuals, couples, or groups. The experience is smooth and exhilarating, combining the excitement of flying with the peacefulness of soaring above the water.

Aside from jet skiing and parasailing, Playa de Palma also offers a variety of **other watersports**, including **banana boat rides, flyboarding, paddleboarding, and wakeboarding**. Rental stations and activity centers are scattered along the beach, and many hotels and resorts offer watersports packages as part of their services.

With its **prime location, excellent facilities, and variety of adrenaline-filled activities**, Playa de Palma is one of the places in Mallorca for **thrill-seekers and adventure lovers**. Whether you're racing across the water on a **jet ski** or floating high above the beach on a **parasail**, this dynamic beachfront promises an **unforgettable watersports experience**.

Cala d'Or (Kayaking & Stand-Up Paddleboarding)
Address: Kayak Mallorca, Carrer de s'Espalmador, 07660 Cala d'Or, Illes Balears, Spain

Cala d'Or, located on the **southeastern coast of Mallorca**, is one of the island's most scenic coastal areas, famous for its **turquoise waters, hidden coves, and picturesque whitewashed buildings**. This resort town is a top destination for **kayaking and stand-up paddleboarding (SUP)**, thanks to its **calm sea conditions, stunning coastal cliffs, and numerous small bays (calas) for exploring**.

The coastline around Cala d'Or is characterized by **a series of sheltered inlets, sea caves, and rocky cliffs**, making it an ideal spot for **kayakers and paddleboarders of all skill levels**. The water here is **typically calm and clear**, allowing for easy navigation and great visibility of **marine life, underwater rock formations, and sandy seabeds**.

One of the things about kayaking and SUP in Cala d'Or is the ability to access **hidden beaches and secluded coves** that are otherwise difficult to reach by foot or car. Some of the most popular spots to explore include:

Cala Gran – The main beach of Cala d'Or, offering a starting point for kayakers and paddleboarders heading towards more secluded areas.

Cala Esmeralda – Known for its **crystal-clear emerald waters**, this small cove is a great place to stop for a swim.

Cala Ferrera – A peaceful and picturesque bay, ideal for beginner paddleboarders.

Cala Mitjana – A secluded and untouched cove surrounded by cliffs, only accessible by **boat, kayak, or SUP**.

Cala Mondragó & Cala S'Amarador – Located within **Mondragó Natural Park**, these beaches are **for a longer kayaking adventure**, with breathtaking scenery along the way.

Kayak and paddleboard rentals are available at **various beachfront locations, water sports centers, and hotels** around Cala d'Or. Many providers offer **guided tours**, where experienced instructors lead paddlers through the **coastal routes, sea caves, and snorkeling spots**. These excursions often include breaks for **swimming, snorkeling, and even cliff jumping**, allowing visitors to fully immerse themselves in the natural beauty of the area.

Stand-up paddleboarding is particularly popular in Cala d'Or due to the **calm water conditions**, making it an accessible activity for **beginners and experienced paddlers alike**. The region's **stunning sunrise and sunset views** also make it a fantastic location for **early morning or late evening paddling sessions**, where the **sea is at its most peaceful and the light enhances the beauty of the coastline**.

In addition to kayaking and SUP, Cala d'Or is a great spot for **snorkeling**, with numerous underwater caves and vibrant marine life, including **colorful fish, octopuses, and sea stars**. Many kayak and SUP tours include snorkeling stops, allowing adventurers to explore beneath the surface as well.

Cala d'Or's combination of **scenic coastal landscapes, crystal-clear waters, and accessible water conditions** makes it one of the **locations in Mallorca** for kayaking and stand-up paddleboarding. Whether you're looking for a **relaxing paddle along the coast**, an **adventure exploring hidden sea caves**, or a **sunset SUP session**, this stunning destination offers an **unforgettable experience on the water**.

Cabrera National Park (Scuba Diving & Boat Trips)
Address: Big Blue Diving, Carrer Martín Ros García, 6, 07181 Palmanova, Illes Balears, Spain

Cabrera National Park, also known as **Parc Nacional Marítim-Terrestre de l'Arxipèlag de Cabrera**, is one of the most pristine and ecologically rich areas in the Balearic Islands. Located **about 10 kilometers (6 miles) south of Mallorca**, this **protected marine and land reserve** consists of a main island, Cabrera, and **18**

smaller islets, forming a **biodiversity hotspot with crystal-clear waters, underwater caves, and untouched landscapes**. It is one of the **destinations in Mallorca for scuba diving and boat trips**, offering visitors a chance to explore an **unspoiled Mediterranean paradise**.

As a **national park since 1991**, Cabrera has been **strictly protected from mass tourism and development**, preserving its **diverse marine and terrestrial ecosystems**. The waters surrounding the islands are among the **cleanest and clearest in the Mediterranean**, making them **ideal for scuba diving and snorkeling**. Divers can explore **seagrass meadows, underwater cliffs, and vibrant coral formations**, where a rich variety of marine life thrives. Cabrera's marine biodiversity includes **groupers, moray eels, octopuses, barracudas, rays, sea turtles, and even dolphins**. Occasionally, **whale species such as fin whales** are spotted passing through the deeper waters of the park.

One of the most famous diving sites in Cabrera is the **Cova Blava (Blue Cave)**, a mesmerizing sea cave that is illuminated by **natural sunlight reflecting off the seabed**, creating an intense blue glow inside the cave. Many boat tours make a stop here, allowing visitors to **swim and snorkel** in its breathtaking waters. The cave is visited in the afternoon, when the light is at its peak and creates the most spectacular blue hues.

Scuba diving in Cabrera requires a **special permit**, as the park has strict conservation regulations to protect its marine life. Only a limited number of divers are allowed per day, ensuring the underwater ecosystem remains undisturbed. Several diving centers in Mallorca, particularly in **Palma, Colònia de Sant Jordi, and Port de Andratx**, offer **guided diving excursions** to Cabrera, providing equipment rental and professional dive guides.

For those who prefer to **stay above the water, boat trips** to Cabrera offer an incredible way to experience the park's natural beauty. Boats depart from **Colònia de Sant Jordi**, the closest port on Mallorca's southern coast, with journeys taking around **30 to 45 minutes**. Most tours include **stops for swimming, snorkeling, and sightseeing**, allowing visitors to take in **the rugged cliffs, hidden beaches, and historic sites** on the island. One of the main attractions is the **Castle of Cabrera**, a **14th-century fortress** perched on a hill overlooking the main bay, which once served as a watchtower to defend against pirate attacks.

Hiking is another popular activity for visitors to Cabrera. There are several marked trails that lead to **scenic viewpoints, birdwatching areas, and secluded beaches**, offering a chance to explore the island's **untouched nature**. Cabrera is home to **over 150 species of birds**, including the **Balearic shearwater, peregrine falcon, and Audouin's gull**, making it an excellent destination for **birdwatchers and nature lovers**.

Because Cabrera is a **protected area**, there are no hotels or permanent accommodations on the island, making it a **true escape into nature**. However, visitors can stay in Mallorca and take **day trips** or, in some cases, **obtain special permits to camp overnight**. The national park authority regulates access to ensure the preservation of the fragile ecosystem.

Cabrera National Park offers a **rare opportunity to experience the Mediterranean in its most natural state**, free from modern development and human impact. Whether exploring its **underwater world through scuba diving, enjoying a boat trip along its pristine coastline, or hiking to breathtaking viewpoints**, Cabrera provides an **unforgettable adventure** for nature lovers, divers, and anyone looking for a **peaceful escape from Mallorca's busier tourist spots**.

III. CYCLING ROUTES

Sa Calobra – The Iconic Climb
Starting Point: Ma-10, 07315 Escorca, Illes Balears, Spain

Sa Calobra is one of the most **legendary cycling routes in Mallorca**, often considered a **bucket-list climb** for cyclists worldwide. Located in the **Serra de Tramuntana**, a UNESCO World Heritage Site, this **stunning yet challenging ascent** is famous for its **steep gradients, breathtaking switchbacks, and the iconic "Tie Knot" hairpin bend** that makes it one of the most thrilling rides in Europe.

The route starts at **sea level in the small coastal village of Sa Calobra** and climbs **9.5 kilometers (5.9 miles) with an average gradient of 7%**, reaching a maximum elevation of **682 meters (2,238 feet)**. The toughest sections reach gradients of **up to 12%**, making it a physically demanding yet rewarding climb. The climb is unique because cyclists **must first descend before ascending**, meaning once you reach the bottom, the only way out is to ride back up.

The road to Sa Calobra, officially known as **Ma-2141**, was designed by **Italian engineer Antonio Parietti** in the 1930s and is famous for its **12 hairpin turns** and the **incredible 270-degree "Nus de sa Corbata" (Tie Knot Bend)**, where the road loops around itself in a spectacular twist. This section provides **stunning aerial views** of the winding road below and is one of the most photographed cycling spots in Mallorca.

The **ride experience** is both thrilling and demanding. The initial **descent into Sa Calobra** is technical, requiring careful braking and handling, as the road is **narrow with sharp corners**. Once at the bottom, cyclists take a brief rest in the **seaside village**, which has **cafés and restaurants** where riders can refuel before beginning the demanding ascent. The climb itself is relentless, with **few opportunities to rest**, and requires a steady pace to maintain endurance.

One of the highlights of Sa Calobra is the **stunning scenery**, which includes **sheer limestone cliffs, rugged rock formations, and**

panoramic sea views. The landscape constantly changes as cyclists ascend, passing through **pine forests, dramatic ravines, and open mountain vistas**.

Due to its popularity, the road can get **busy with cars, tour buses, and other cyclists**, especially during **peak cycling season (March to May and September to October)**. Many cyclists start **early in the morning to avoid traffic** and experience the climb in quieter conditions.

Sa Calobra is often included in **professional training routes**, including the **Mallorca 312 cycling event**, and has been used by top pro riders, including Team Sky (now INEOS Grenadiers), as part of their pre-season training. The **physical challenge, combined with breathtaking views and iconic switchbacks**, makes Sa Calobra a **must-ride climb for serious cyclists visiting Mallorca**.

For those looking for an **alternative approach**, some cyclists choose to **take a boat from Port de Sóller to Sa Calobra**, allowing them to **avoid the descent and start directly from sea level**, making the climb even more rewarding.

With its **unforgettable challenge, world-class road quality, and stunning mountain scenery**, Sa Calobra remains **one of the most famous and rewarding cycling routes in Mallorca**, offering an experience that is both **grueling and exhilarating**.

Cap de Formentor – Scenic Coastal Ride
Starting Point: Pollença, 07460 Pollença, Illes Balears, Spain

Cap de Formentor is one of the most **spectacular and scenic cycling routes in Mallorca**, offering **breathtaking coastal views, dramatic cliffs, and winding mountain roads** that lead to the **northernmost point of the island**. Often referred to as the **"Lighthouse Route,"** this ride is a favorite among **cyclists, photographers, and nature lovers**, providing an unforgettable experience of Mallorca's rugged beauty.

The route begins in **Pollença**, a charming town known for its **cobbled streets, historic architecture, and cycling-friendly atmosphere**. From here, riders head toward the **Ma-2210 road**, which leads through the **Formentor Peninsula**, a stunning region of the **Serra de Tramuntana** mountain range. The total distance from

Pollença to the **Formentor Lighthouse (Far de Formentor)** is approximately **20 kilometers (12.4 miles) one way**, making it a **moderate-to-challenging ride** depending on weather conditions and wind strength.

The ride features **rolling hills, technical descents, and steady climbs**, with a total elevation gain of around **900 meters (2,950 feet)**. One of the most challenging sections is the **initial climb from Pollença to Mirador Es Colomer**, a **3.5-kilometer ascent with an average gradient of 6%**, reaching an elevation of **232 meters (761 feet)**. At the top, cyclists are rewarded with **breathtaking panoramic views** of the **Formentor cliffs, the Bay of Pollença, and the Mediterranean Sea**. The **Es Colomer viewpoint** is one of the most famous photo spots in Mallorca, often visited by cyclists and tourists alike.

After Mirador Es Colomer, the road continues through **pine forests and limestone cliffs**, with thrilling descents and winding turns. The **second climb near the Formentor Beach area** is another challenging section, leading cyclists toward **secluded coves and pristine beaches** with **crystal-clear turquoise waters**. Some riders take a break at **Formentor Beach**, a stunning stretch of white sand surrounded by lush pine trees, before continuing toward the lighthouse.

The final stretch to **Formentor Lighthouse** is one of the most **exhilarating and challenging** parts of the ride. This **8-kilometer section features sharp hairpin bends, narrow roads, and strong coastal winds**, making it a **technical and demanding** ride, especially for less-experienced cyclists. However, the **reward at the end** is a **breathtaking 360-degree view** from the **Formentor Lighthouse**, which stands **210 meters (689 feet) above the sea**, overlooking the dramatic cliffs and endless blue waters.

Because the **Formentor Peninsula is a protected area**, traffic regulations apply during peak seasons. From **June to September, private vehicles are restricted**, and cyclists share the road primarily with **shuttle buses and fellow riders**, making it a **much safer and more enjoyable experience**. However, it is recommended to start early in the morning or late in the afternoon to **avoid strong winds and crowds**.

Cap de Formentor is a route that combines **physical endurance with stunning natural scenery**, making it one of the **most**

rewarding cycling experiences in Mallorca. Whether for the **challenge of the climbs, the thrill of the descents, or the beauty of the coastline**, this ride offers an **unforgettable journey through one of the island's most spectacular landscapes**.

Palma to Andratx – A Classic Road Ride
Starting Point: Palma, 07001 Palma, Illes Balears, Spain

The **Palma to Andratx** cycling route is a **classic road ride** in Mallorca, offering a **mix of coastal scenery, rolling hills, and challenging climbs**. This **65-kilometer (40-mile) route** is one of the most popular among both amateur and professional cyclists, providing **stunning Mediterranean views, charming villages, and smooth asphalt roads**. It is known for being a **scenic yet manageable ride**, making it an excellent choice for cyclists looking to experience **Mallorca's diverse landscapes without tackling the extreme climbs of the Tramuntana range**.

The route begins in **Palma**, Mallorca's capital, and follows the **MA-1 coastal road**, heading southwest toward **Andratx**, a beautiful town nestled in the foothills of the **Serra de Tramuntana**. The ride starts off relatively **flat and smooth**, allowing cyclists to enjoy the **coastal breeze and sea views** while warming up their legs.

After passing **Calvià**, the terrain begins to feature **rolling hills**, offering a mix of **short climbs and fast descents**. The **first notable climb** comes near **Costa de la Calma**, where riders gain elevation while enjoying **panoramic views of the Mediterranean coastline**. The ascent is steady and not too steep, making it an ideal challenge for **intermediate-level cyclists**.

As the ride continues, cyclists pass through **picturesque coastal villages**, including **Santa Ponsa and Peguera**, both popular resort towns known for their **beautiful beaches and relaxed atmosphere**. These towns provide excellent spots to stop for **a quick coffee or snack**, with plenty of cafés catering to cyclists.

One of the highlights of the route is the **section between Camp de Mar and Andratx**, where the **roads become more winding and scenic**, surrounded by **pine forests, rugged cliffs, and terraced hillsides**. The descent into Andratx is exhilarating, offering **sweeping curves and smooth tarmac** that make for a thrilling ride.

Upon reaching **Andratx**, cyclists can explore the town's **historic streets, traditional cafés, and relaxed ambiance** before deciding whether to continue further or return to Palma. Many riders extend their journey to **Port d'Andratx**, a picturesque harbor just a few kilometers away, where **seaside restaurants and waterfront cafés** offer the setting for a post-ride meal.

For those looking for **a longer challenge**, the route can be extended into the **Serra de Tramuntana**, heading toward **Estellencs and Banyalbufar**, where the terrain becomes more mountainous with **steeper climbs and dramatic coastal scenery**.

Because this is a **well-traveled cycling route**, road conditions are excellent, and there are plenty of places for **water and rest stops** along the way. The ride is enjoyed **early in the morning or late afternoon**, as traffic can get heavier on the main roads during peak tourist seasons.

The **Palma to Andratx ride** is ideal for cyclists seeking a **balance of distance, elevation, and breathtaking views** without the extreme gradients found in Mallorca's more mountainous routes. With its **stunning coastal scenery, smooth roads, and charming**

towns, this ride offers an **unforgettable cycling experience** that showcases the **thrill of Mallorca's southwestern coastline**.

IV. BOAT TOURS & ISLAND HOPPING

Cabrera National Park Boat Tour
Departure: Puerto de Colònia de Sant Jordi, 07638 Colònia de Sant Jordi, Illes Balears, Spain

The Cabrera National Park Boat Tour is one of the most breathtaking island-hopping experiences in Mallorca, taking visitors to the pristine Cabrera Archipelago, a protected marine and land reserve located 10 km south of Mallorca's coast. This unspoiled paradise consists of a main island, Cabrera, and 18 smaller islets, offering an extraordinary mix of natural beauty, rich marine biodiversity, and historical landmarks. The park's restricted access and conservation status ensure that it remains a secluded and untouched gem of the Mediterranean.

The boat tour departs from Colònia de Sant Jordi, a small coastal town on Mallorca's southern coast, and takes approximately 30-45 minutes to reach Cabrera. The journey itself is scenic and relaxing, with opportunities to spot dolphins, seabirds, and other marine life along the way. Most tours operate on speedboats, sailboats, or catamarans, providing different levels of comfort and adventure.

Upon arrival, visitors disembark at Cabrera Island, where they can explore its stunning coastline, hiking trails, and hidden beaches. The island is completely uninhabited except for a small ranger station and a historical military outpost, making it a true escape into nature. There are several key highlights on the island:

Cabrera Castle – A 14th-century fortress perched on a hill overlooking the main bay, originally built to protect against pirate attacks. The short hike to the top offers spectacular panoramic views of the island and surrounding waters.

Hiking Trails – The island features several well-marked trails that lead to secluded beaches, lighthouses, and viewpoints, offering a chance to experience Cabrera's unspoiled Mediterranean landscape.

Es Port Beach – A small, crystal-clear bay for swimming and snorkeling, surrounded by rocky cliffs and pine trees.

One of the most iconic moments of the tour is the visit to Cova Blava (Blue Cave), a stunning sea cave that glows with brilliant shades of blue when sunlight reflects off the seabed. Most boat tours stop here for a swim, allowing visitors to experience the magical color effects of the water firsthand.

Snorkeling in Cabrera is exceptional, as the protected marine park is home to a diverse range of fish, octopuses, starfish, and even sea turtles. Due to its conservation status, fishing and anchoring are strictly prohibited, ensuring that the waters remain pristine and full of marine life.

Most tours last around 5-6 hours, including travel time, exploration, and swimming breaks. Visitors are encouraged to bring sunscreen, water, and comfortable walking shoes, as there are no shops or restaurants on the island, preserving its natural and untouched environment.

Because access to Cabrera is strictly limited, it is essential to book boat tours in advance, especially during the peak season (May to September). Only a small number of visitors are allowed per day to minimize environmental impact.

The Cabrera National Park Boat Tour offers an unforgettable experience of Mallorca's most preserved natural area, combining adventure, relaxation, and ecological discovery. Whether hiking to the castle, snorkeling in crystal-clear waters, or swimming in the Blue Cave, this tour provides a once-in-a-lifetime opportunity to explore one of the Mediterranean's last true hidden gems.

Dragonera Island Boat Excursion
Departure: Port d'Andratx, 07157 Andratx, Illes Balears, Spain

The Dragonera Island Boat Excursion is a must-do experience for visitors looking to explore one of Mallorca's most unspoiled natural areas. Sa Dragonera, a small, uninhabited island located off the southwestern coast of Mallorca, is part of the Parc Natural de sa Dragonera, a protected natural park known for its rugged landscapes, rich biodiversity, and fascinating history. The island gets its name from its dragon-like shape, and it is famous for its stunning cliffs, hiking trails, and resident Balearic lizards, which are unique to the region.

The boat trip to Dragonera Island departs from Port d'Andratx, Sant Elm, or Peguera, with journeys taking about 15-30 minutes, depending on the departure point. Along the way, passengers are treated to breathtaking views of the Mallorcan coastline, with its hidden coves, dramatic cliffs, and crystal-clear waters. Many tours also include stops at nearby secluded beaches and snorkeling spots before reaching Dragonera.

Upon arrival, visitors can explore the island's four well-marked hiking trails, each leading to different parts of the island and offering spectacular views:

Camí des Far Vell: A short and easy walk leading to the ruins of the old lighthouse, with panoramic views of the Mediterranean.

Camí de Na Pòpia: A moderate-to-challenging hike to the highest point on the island (353 meters / 1,158 feet), where the remains of an old watchtower and lighthouse provide a historic insight into the island's past.

Camí de Llevant: A scenic coastal path leading to beautiful rock formations and secluded bays, for photography.

Camí de Tramuntana: A longer and more adventurous hike that showcases cliffs, caves, and spectacular sea views.

The island's wildlife is another major highlight. Sa Dragonera is home to thousands of Balearic lizards (Podarcis lilfordi), which are endemic to the Balearic Islands and have adapted to the unique environment of the island. Visitors will also see seabirds such as Audouin's gulls, peregrine falcons, and cormorants, making it a great spot for birdwatching.

The waters surrounding Dragonera are part of a marine reserve, making it a fantastic location for snorkeling and diving. Many boat excursions offer snorkeling equipment so visitors can explore the crystal-clear waters, rich with colorful fish, sea sponges, and coral formations.

For history enthusiasts, Dragonera has a fascinating past. It was once a pirate hideout, and historical records mention famous pirates such as Barbarossa using the island as a base in the 16th century. Later, it served as a military outpost and lighthouse station, remnants of which can still be seen today.

Since Dragonera is a protected natural park, no permanent buildings, restaurants, or shops exist on the island, keeping it untouched and preserved. Visitors must bring water, snacks, and appropriate hiking shoes, as the terrain can be rocky and exposed to the sun.

Most tours last between 3 to 5 hours, giving visitors ample time to hike, explore, swim, and snorkel before returning to Mallorca. Boat trips are available year-round, but the favourable time to visit is from April to October, when the weather is ideal for hiking and swimming.

The Dragonera Island Boat Excursion offers a mix of adventure, history, and natural beauty, making it an unforgettable experience for hikers, nature lovers, and snorkelers. Whether you want to climb to the highest peak for breathtaking views, explore hidden coves, or encounter rare wildlife, Dragonera provides a unique and immersive escape into Mallorca's wild side.

Catamaran Cruise to Formentor Beach & Lighthouse
Departure: Port de Pollença, 07470 Pollença, Illes Balears, Spain

The **Catamaran Cruise to Formentor Beach & Lighthouse** is one of the most **picturesque and relaxing boat trips in Mallorca**, offering **breathtaking coastal views, crystal-clear waters, and access to one of the island's most beautiful beaches**. Located on the **northern coast of Mallorca**, the **Formentor Peninsula** is famous for its **rugged cliffs, pristine beaches, and scenic hiking trails**, making it an ideal destination for a **catamaran excursion**.

The tour typically **departs from Port de Pollença**, a charming seaside town known for its **marina, waterfront promenade, and traditional Mediterranean charm**. From the moment the catamaran sets sail, passengers are treated to **spectacular panoramic views of the Tramuntana mountain range, hidden coves, and the open blue waters of the Mediterranean**. The **tranquil pace of the catamaran** allows visitors to fully soak in the **stunning natural surroundings** while enjoying the **sea breeze and sunshine**.

During the journey, the catamaran makes **stops at several secluded spots**, where passengers can **swim, snorkel, and sunbathe** in the **crystal-clear waters**. The **Formentor coastline** is home to **rich marine life, coral reefs, and underwater rock formations**, making it a great spot for **snorkeling**. Many catamarans are equipped with **snorkeling gear, paddleboards, and sometimes even underwater scooters**, allowing guests to explore the **vibrant underwater world**.

One of the main highlights of the cruise is the visit to **Formentor Beach (Platja de Formentor)**, a stunning **white-sand beach lined with pine trees and surrounded by dramatic cliffs**. Known for its **turquoise waters and soft golden sand**, Formentor Beach is considered one of the **most beautiful beaches in Mallorca**. Guests can relax on the beach, take a refreshing swim, or walk along the shore while enjoying the **breathtaking views of the mountains and sea**.

After spending time at the beach, the catamaran continues toward the **Formentor Lighthouse (Far de Formentor)**, located at the **northernmost tip of Mallorca**. This iconic lighthouse, built in **1863**, sits atop a **210-meter-high (689 feet) cliff**, offering **spectacular 360-degree views** of the **Mediterranean Sea and the Tramuntana coastline**. The journey to the lighthouse is particularly scenic, as the catamaran navigates past **steep cliffs, rocky formations, and dramatic sea caves**. In some tours, guests can enjoy **a guided commentary** on the **history and significance of the lighthouse**, as well as insights into the local **wildlife and marine ecosystem**.

Many **luxury catamarans** include onboard amenities such as **buffet-style Mediterranean lunches, drinks, and sunbathing decks**, making the cruise a **relaxing and indulgent experience**. Some also offer **sunset cruises**, where guests can witness the **breathtaking golden hues of the sunset over the Tramuntana mountains**, creating a truly **magical atmosphere**.

The entire cruise typically lasts **4 to 6 hours**, depending on the itinerary and stops included. Most catamaran operators provide **round-trip transport from nearby hotels**, making it easy for visitors staying in **Alcúdia, Pollença, or Port de Sóller** to join the excursion.

The **Catamaran Cruise to Formentor Beach & Lighthouse** is for those seeking a **relaxing yet adventurous experience**, offering a **combination of beach time, snorkeling, breathtaking landscapes, and sailing along one of Mallorca's most stunning coastlines**. Whether you're looking for a **romantic getaway, a family-friendly excursion, or simply a day of luxury on the water**, this tour provides an **unforgettable way to explore the beauty of northern Mallorca**.

Palma Bay Sunset & Coastal Cruise
Departure: Moll Vell, 07012 Palma, Illes Balears, Spain

The **Palma Bay Sunset & Coastal Cruise** is one of the most **relaxing and scenic boat experiences** in Mallorca, offering passengers a chance to **sail along the stunning coastline of Palma Bay while witnessing a breathtaking Mediterranean sunset**. This cruise is for those seeking a **romantic evening, a fun social outing, or a peaceful escape from the city's bustling streets**. Departing from **Moll Vell in Palma's Marina**, this cruise provides **spectacular views of Palma's skyline, historic landmarks, and the open sea**.

As the catamaran or yacht sets sail, passengers can enjoy **panoramic views of the iconic landmarks of Palma**, including the **La Seu Cathedral (Palma Cathedral), Bellver Castle, and the Almudaina Palace**. The calm waters of Palma Bay, combined with the golden hues of the setting sun, create a **picture- backdrop for photography and relaxation**.

Most sunset cruises **last between 2.5 to 4 hours**, allowing passengers ample time to **soak in the beauty of the coastline, swim in secluded coves, and enjoy onboard entertainment**. Many operators include **stops at tranquil bays**, such as **Cala Blava or Illetas**, where guests can take a **refreshing dip in the crystal-clear waters** or snorkel among vibrant marine life.

One of the highlights of the **Palma Bay Sunset Cruise** is the onboard experience. Many boats feature **live music, DJ performances, or ambient lounge music**, creating a **laid-back and enjoyable atmosphere**. Guests can **relax on deck with a cocktail in hand**, enjoying the **warm Mediterranean breeze** as the sun sets over the horizon.

Catering varies depending on the tour, with some cruises offering **a gourmet buffet, traditional Mallorcan tapas, or BBQ-style dining**. Many also include **complimentary drinks such as sangria, wine, or cava**, adding to the indulgent experience.

For those looking for a more **exclusive experience**, luxury yacht charters are available, providing **a more private and intimate setting** with personalized service, fine dining, and premium drinks.

These options are popular for **special occasions such as anniversaries, birthdays, and proposals**.

The **favourable time for the Palma Bay Sunset Cruise** is during the **spring and summer months (April to October)**, when the **weather is warm, and the sea conditions are ideal for sailing**. However, sunset cruises are also available in the **off-season**, offering a more **peaceful and uncrowded experience**.

The **Palma Bay Sunset & Coastal Cruise** is an **unforgettable way to experience the magic of Mallorca's coastline**, combining **stunning views, relaxation, music, and great food**. Whether you're looking to **celebrate a special occasion, enjoy a romantic evening, or simply unwind with friends**, this cruise provides a sweet **ending to a day in paradise**.

V. GOLFING IN MALLORCA

Golf Son Gual
Address: Ma-15, Km 11.5, 07199 Palma, Illes Balears, Spain

Golfing in Mallorca is one of the island's premier activities, attracting players from around the world due to its **spectacular**

golf courses, year-round mild climate, and stunning Mediterranean scenery. With over 20 high-quality golf courses, Mallorca offers a variety of options for both casual golfers and experienced players, making it one of the golf destinations in Europe.

Mallorca's golf courses are known for their beautiful landscapes, challenging layouts, and top-tier facilities. Many courses are set against breathtaking backdrops, including coastal cliffs, rolling hills, and views of the Tramuntana mountains, providing an unforgettable golfing experience. The island's golf courses are also strategically located, with many of them near luxury resorts, beaches, and historic towns, allowing visitors to combine golf with relaxation and sightseeing.

One of the most renowned golf courses in Mallorca is Golf Son Gual, located just 15 minutes from Palma. It is a championship-level course, often regarded as one of the in Spain. Designed for experienced players, it features immaculate fairways, large greens, and numerous water hazards, creating a challenging yet rewarding round of golf. The course is exclusive and limited in daily players, ensuring an **uncrowded and high-quality experience**.

Another **popular course** is **Golf Son Vida**, the **oldest golf course in Mallorca**, opened in 1964. Located in **Palma's prestigious Son Vida area**, this course has hosted **several European Tour events** and is known for its **historic charm and well-maintained greens**. It offers a **balanced challenge**, with **tree-lined fairways, elevation changes, and scenic views of Palma Bay**.

For golfers seeking a **picturesque coastal experience, Alcanada Golf Club**, located in the **north of Mallorca near Alcúdia**, is a standout choice. Designed by **Robert Trent Jones Jr.**, this course offers **incredible sea views** with holes that run alongside the **Mediterranean coast**, creating a **stunning setting for a round of golf**. The course is known for its **strategic layout and fast greens**, appealing to both **amateurs and professionals**.

Another highly rated option is **T Golf & Country Club Poniente**, located in **Calvià, near Magaluf and Santa Ponsa**. This **18-hole championship course** is known for its **wide fairways, large bunkers, and rolling terrain**, offering a **fun yet challenging round** for all skill levels. After a recent renovation, the course now features **modern facilities, a stylish clubhouse, and a top-tier restaurant**, making it a favorite among golf enthusiasts.

For those looking for **a more relaxed and scenic golfing experience, Pula Golf Resort** in **Son Servera** is an excellent choice. This **par-72 course** was redesigned by **José María Olazábal** to meet **PGA Tour standards**, making it a popular venue for **professional tournaments**. It also features **a beautiful hotel and wellness center**, allowing golfers to enjoy **a complete luxury golf getaway**.

Mallorca's golf courses **cater to all types of players**, from **beginners looking for easy courses** to **advanced golfers seeking challenging layouts**. Most courses offer **driving ranges, practice greens, golf academies, and club rentals**, ensuring a **convenient and enjoyable experience** for visitors who may not have brought their own equipment.

The favourable time to golf in Mallorca is **spring (March to May) and autumn (September to November)**, when the **weather is warm but not too hot**, and the **courses are less crowded** than in the peak summer months. However, thanks to Mallorca's **mild Mediterranean climate**, golf is **a year-round activity**, even in **winter**, when temperatures are still comfortable.

Beyond the courses themselves, Mallorca offers **luxury golf resorts, fine dining, and excellent clubhouses**, making it an ideal **golfing holiday destination**. Many courses also host **corporate events, private tournaments, and golf training camps**, attracting professionals and enthusiasts from all over Europe.

With its **exceptional golf courses, breathtaking scenery, and world-class facilities**, Mallorca is a **golfer's paradise** that combines **sport, nature, and relaxation in one unforgettable experience**. Whether you are **a seasoned player looking for a challenging round or a beginner wanting to enjoy a casual game in a stunning setting**, golfing in Mallorca promises to be an **unmatched experience on one of the most beautiful islands in the Mediterranean.**

VI. SHOPPING & MARKETS

Mercat de l'Olivar (Palma's Central Market)
Address: Plaça de l'Olivar, 4, 07002 Palma, Illes Balears, Spain

Mercat de l'Olivar is Palma's largest and most vibrant indoor market, offering a true taste of Mallorca's culinary culture. Located in the heart of Palma's Old Town, this bustling market has been a cornerstone of local trade and gastronomy since its opening in 1951. It is one of the places on the island to experience authentic Mallorcan flavors, fresh produce, and traditional delicacies, making it a must-visit destination for both locals and tourists.

Covering two levels, Mercat de l'Olivar is home to over 100 stalls, offering a wide variety of products, including fresh seafood, meats, cheeses, baked goods, fruits, vegetables, wines, and gourmet specialties. The market is divided into different sections, each specializing in a particular type of food:

Seafood Section: One of the most impressive areas of the market, featuring an incredible selection of fresh fish, shellfish, and seafood caught daily from the Mediterranean. Locals and chefs come here early in the morning to buy red prawns from Sóller, lobsters, squid, and sea bass. Some vendors even offer oysters and sushi tasting experiences.

Meat & Charcuterie Section: This area showcases local sausages, cured meats, and high-quality cuts of beef, lamb, and pork. A highlight is the famous Sobrasada de Mallorca, a traditional spicy cured sausage, and Jamon Ibérico, a delicacy in Spanish cuisine.

Fruit & Vegetable Section: Here, visitors can find seasonal produce, organic fruits, Mediterranean herbs, and locally grown vegetables, sourced from Mallorcan farms.

Cheese & Dairy Section: Offers a fantastic selection of local and Spanish cheeses, including Mahón cheese from Menorca, Manchego from the mainland, and artisanal goat cheeses. Many stalls provide cheese tastings, allowing visitors to sample before purchasing.

Bakery & Sweets: Traditional Mallorcan pastries like Ensaimadas (sweet spiral pastries dusted with powdered sugar) and Coca de Patata (soft potato buns) are sold alongside freshly baked bread and handmade chocolates.

Wine & Spirits Section: Features local wines, vermouth, and craft liqueurs like Hierbas de Mallorca, a popular herbal digestive drink. Some stalls offer wine tastings, making it a great place to explore Mallorca's wine culture.

In addition to its fresh food stalls, Mercat de l'Olivar is also known for its gourmet eateries and tapas bars, where visitors can enjoy freshly prepared meals made with market ingredients. From traditional paella and seafood platters to tapas, pintxos, and local delicacies, the market provides a lively atmosphere where people gather to eat and socialize.

Another great feature is the central bar area, where visitors can enjoy a glass of Mallorcan wine, sangria, or fresh juices while taking in the vibrant market scene. Many food stalls allow you to buy fresh ingredients and have them cooked on the spot, offering a unique farm-to-table experience.

The market is open from Monday to Saturday, with the busiest times in the morning as locals and chefs do their shopping. Arriving early ensures the selection of products, while visiting around midday is ideal for enjoying a tapas-style lunch.

Located just a short walk from Plaça Major and Palma Cathedral, Mercat de l'Olivar is not just a place to shop but an essential cultural and culinary experience in Mallorca. Whether you're looking to buy fresh local ingredients, taste gourmet specialties, or enjoy a lively tapas experience, this market offers an authentic and flavorful insight into the island's gastronomic traditions.

Paseo del Borne (Luxury Shopping & Boutiques)
Address: Passeig del Born, 07012 Palma, Illes Balears, Spain

Paseo del Borne, often referred to as "The Golden Mile" of Palma, is Mallorca's most prestigious shopping street, renowned for its luxury boutiques, high-end brands, and elegant ambiance. Located in the heart of Palma's Old Town, this tree-lined boulevard stretches between Plaza de Juan Carlos I and Plaza de la Reina, offering a blend of history, fashion, and upscale shopping.

The boulevard is flanked by majestic historic buildings, grand stone benches, and stylish street lamps, creating an atmospheric setting reminiscent of the grand avenues of Paris and Barcelona. Originally built in the 19th century on what was once a medieval water channel, Paseo del Borne has become a prime shopping destination for luxury fashion, designer labels, and exclusive jewelry stores.

Shoppers can find some of the world's most famous luxury brands along Paseo del Borne, including:

Louis Vuitton – The iconic French fashion house, offering its latest collections of handbags, shoes, and accessories.

Cartier – A symbol of elegance and sophistication, featuring exquisite watches, fine jewelry, and luxury accessories.

Rolex & Relojería Alemana – A high-end watch boutique selling prestigious timepieces from brands like Rolex, Patek Philippe, and Audemars Piguet.

Carolina Herrera – A designer boutique showcasing elegant women's fashion, handbags, and fragrances.

Hugo Boss – A store specializing in premium men's and women's fashion, from tailored suits to casual wear.

Massimo Dutti & Zara Home – Part of the Spanish Inditex group, offering high-quality fashion and stylish home decor.

In addition to international luxury brands, Paseo del Borne is home to exclusive Spanish and Mallorcan designers, including Camper

(Mallorca's famous footwear brand), Relojería Alemana (a family-run luxury watch store), and jewelry boutiques featuring Mallorca's renowned pearls.

Beyond shopping, Paseo del Borne is also known for its chic cafés, trendy restaurants, and stylish cocktail bars, making it a place to relax after a shopping spree. Some of the most popular spots include:

Cappuccino Grand Café - A sophisticated café known for its premium coffee, gourmet breakfasts, and people-watching atmosphere.

Rialto Living - A concept store featuring fashion, home decor, art, and an elegant café with Mediterranean-inspired dishes.

Bar Bosch - A historic café with a terrace, famous for its "Llonguets" (Mallorcan sandwiches) and traditional Spanish tapas.

Paseo del Borne is not just a shopping destination, but also a cultural and social hub. Throughout the year, it hosts fashion events, outdoor exhibitions, and festive decorations, particularly during Christmas, when the street is beautifully illuminated.

The boulevard is also located near some of Palma's most iconic landmarks, including Palma Cathedral (La Seu), Almudaina Palace, and the historic La Lonja district, making it easy to combine a day of shopping with sightseeing.

For those looking to experience luxury, elegance, and designer shopping in Mallorca, Paseo del Borne is the essential destination. Whether browsing high-end boutiques, indulging in fine dining, or simply soaking up the stylish atmosphere, this boulevard offers a refined and glamorous shopping experience in the heart of Palma.

Inca Market (Traditional Weekly Market)
Address: Avinguda del General Luque, 07300 Inca, Illes Balears, Spain

Inca Market is the largest and most famous traditional weekly market in Mallorca, held every Thursday in the town of Inca, located in the center of the island. This vibrant outdoor market has been a major commercial hub for centuries, attracting locals and tourists alike who come to explore its wide variety of products, from handcrafted leather goods and artisan crafts to fresh local produce and traditional Mallorcan specialties.

Inca is historically known as Mallorca's leather capital, and the market reflects this heritage with numerous stalls selling handmade leather goods, including jackets, shoes, belts, handbags, and wallets. Many of these products are made by local artisans, using traditional techniques that have been passed down for generations. Some of the most famous Mallorcan leather brands, such as Camper and Lotusse, have their origins in Inca, and visitors can often find factory outlet stores nearby offering discounts on high-quality leather products.

Beyond leather, Inca Market is a treasure trove of authentic Mallorcan goods, including:

Handmade ceramics and pottery – Beautifully designed plates, bowls, and tiles with traditional Mediterranean patterns.

Textiles and fabrics – Known as "Robes de Llengües", these brightly colored woven fabrics are unique to Mallorca and are used for home décor, bags, and cushions.

Jewelry and accessories – Featuring handcrafted pearl jewelry from Mallorca, as well as silver and gold pieces made by local artisans.

Baskets and woven goods – Handwoven straw baskets, hats, and bags, for a sustainable and stylish souvenir.

The food section of the market is a highlight, offering a rich selection of fresh and organic local produce, including:

Seasonal fruits and vegetables – Grown by local farmers, ensuring freshness and quality.

Cured meats and cheeses – Including Sobrasada de Mallorca (a spicy, spreadable pork sausage) and Mahón cheese from Menorca.

Olives and olive oil – High-quality extra virgin olive oil from local Mallorcan groves, often available for tasting.

Traditional sweets and pastries – Such as Ensaimadas, the famous spiral-shaped pastry dusted with powdered sugar.

Local wines and liqueurs – Featuring wines from Mallorca's Binissalem region and traditional herbal liqueurs like Hierbas Mallorquinas.

In addition to shopping, Inca Market is a social and cultural event, with live music, street performers, and local artisans demonstrating their crafts. Many visitors enjoy stopping at the local cafés and tapas bars around the market, sampling dishes like pa amb oli (bread with olive oil, tomatoes, and cured meats) or enjoying a glass of Mallorcan wine.

Because Inca Market is very popular, it's to arrive early in the morning (between 8:00 AM and 10:00 AM) to avoid the busiest crowds. The market spreads throughout the main streets and squares of Inca, especially around Plaza Mallorca and Avinguda del General Luque, with stalls lining the streets and creating a bustling, colorful atmosphere.

For those traveling from Palma or other parts of Mallorca, Inca is easily accessible by train, car, or bus, with the train from Palma taking around 30 minutes. Parking can be difficult due to the crowds, so using public transportation is often recommended.

Inca Market is a must-visit for anyone looking to experience Mallorca's local culture, traditions, and artisanal craftsmanship. Whether you're searching for a unique souvenir, delicious local food, or simply want to soak in the lively atmosphere, this market offers an authentic and immersive shopping experience in the heart of the island.

Santa Catalina Market (Mercat de Santa Catalina) is one of **Palma's most vibrant and trendy food markets**, located in the **Santa Catalina district**, a lively and bohemian neighborhood near the city center. As **Palma's oldest market**, it has been a **hub for fresh local produce, gourmet delicacies, and traditional Mallorcan ingredients** for over a century. Today, it is a favorite destination for **food lovers, chefs, and visitors looking to experience authentic Mediterranean flavors** in a dynamic and social atmosphere.

The market is housed in a **traditional indoor hall**, featuring **dozens of stalls selling high-quality products**, including **fresh seafood, organic fruits and vegetables, local meats, cheeses, spices, and artisanal baked goods**. It combines the feel of a **traditional Spanish market** with a **modern and international touch**, making it a hotspot for both **local residents and tourists**.

One of the biggest attractions of Santa Catalina Market is its **exceptional seafood selection**. Since the market is located **near Palma's port**, vendors receive **fresh catches daily**, offering an array of **Mediterranean fish, shrimp, squid, oysters, and octopus**. Some stalls even provide **on-the-spot seafood preparation**, where visitors can enjoy **freshly shucked oysters or grilled prawns with a glass of local white wine**.

The **meat and charcuterie section** showcases **premium cuts of beef, lamb, and pork**, as well as famous **Spanish cured meats**, such as **Jamón Ibérico, chorizo, and Sobrasada de Mallorca**, a soft and spicy cured sausage that is unique to the island. Many butchers offer **homemade sausages and marinated meats**, for those looking to prepare an authentic Mallorcan meal.

The **cheese and dairy section** is another highlight, featuring **a wide variety of local and Spanish cheeses**, including **Mahón cheese from Menorca, Manchego from the mainland, and artisanal goat and sheep cheeses** produced in Mallorca's rural farms. Many vendors provide **tastings**, allowing visitors to sample different flavors before purchasing.

For those interested in **healthy and organic food**, Santa Catalina Market has several stalls specializing in **organic vegetables, dried fruits, nuts, and fresh herbs**. Locally produced **olive oils, honey, and sea salt** from Mallorca are also available, making them souvenirs or gifts.

In addition to shopping for fresh ingredients, visitors can enjoy **ready-to-eat gourmet dishes at the market's tapas bars and food stalls**. Some of the offerings include:

Fresh sushi and sashimi prepared by skilled chefs.

Traditional Spanish tortillas (omelets) made with fresh farm eggs.

Empanadas and croquettes stuffed with meats, seafood, and vegetables.

Pa amb oli, a simple but delicious Mallorcan dish made with **bread, tomato, olive oil, and cured ham or cheese**.

The market also has **wine and liquor stalls**, where visitors can find **local Mallorcan wines, vermouth, and Hierbas de Mallorca**, a traditional herbal liqueur. Some stalls even offer **wine tastings**, allowing guests to explore different regional varieties.

Santa Catalina Market is not just about shopping—it is a **social experience.** Locals gather here to chat, shop, and enjoy a drink at the lively market bars, making it a great place to soak in the **authentic Mediterranean atmosphere.** The surrounding **Santa Catalina neighborhood** is also filled with **trendy cafés, international restaurants, and boutique shops,** making it the area for a **full-day food and cultural experience.**

The market is **open Monday to Saturday from early morning until around 3 PM,** with the busiest hours between **10 AM and noon.** Arriving early ensures the **selection of products,** while visiting later in the morning is ideal for those who want to enjoy a **relaxed lunch with tapas and drinks.**

With its **high-quality food, lively ambiance, and mix of tradition and modernity,** Santa Catalina Market is a **must-visit destination for food lovers exploring Palma.** Whether you're looking for **fresh seafood, gourmet delicacies, or an authentic tapas experience,** this market offers a **taste of Mallorca's rich culinary culture in a vibrant and stylish setting.**

CHAPTER 4: WHERE TO STAY (RECOMMENDED AREAS & BUDGET OPTIONS)

I. PALMA DE MALLORCA (LUXURY & CULTURE)

Address: Passeig del Born, 07012 Palma, Illes Balears, Spain

Palma de Mallorca is the **luxurious and cultural heart** of the Balearic Islands, offering a blend of **historic landmarks, high-end shopping, fine dining, and a vibrant arts scene**. As the **capital city of Mallorca**, Palma seamlessly combines **Mediterranean charm with modern sophistication**, making it a top destination for travelers looking for both **luxury experiences and cultural immersion**.

The city's **historic core** is a masterpiece of **Gothic, Baroque, and Moorish architecture**, with its **crown jewel, La Seu Cathedral (Palma Cathedral), dominating the skyline**. This **magnificent Gothic structure**, built in the 14th century, is one of the **most impressive cathedrals in Spain**, featuring **stunning stained-**

glass windows, towering columns, and artistic renovations by **Antoni Gaudí**. Just next to the cathedral, the **Royal Palace of La Almudaina**, a former Moorish fortress turned royal residence, showcases **centuries of Mallorcan history, royal artifacts, and breathtaking sea views**.

The **Paseo del Borne**, known as **Palma's "Golden Mile,"** is the city's **luxury shopping district**, where visitors can find **high-end boutiques from world-renowned designers** such as **Louis Vuitton, Cartier, Hugo Boss, and Rolex**. This elegant boulevard, lined with **majestic trees, historic buildings, and stylish cafés**, is also home to **exclusive jewelry stores, luxury watchmakers, and Spanish fashion brands** like **Loewe and Massimo Dutti**. Just a short walk away, **Avenida de Jaume III** offers even more **designer stores and upscale department stores**, making it a paradise for luxury shoppers.

Beyond shopping, Palma boasts **some of the finest hotels and resorts in the Mediterranean**, with **luxurious five-star accommodations** such as **Hotel Cappuccino, Sant Francesc Hotel Singular, and Can Bordoy Grand House & Garden**. Many of these **boutique hotels** are housed in **restored historic mansions**, blending **modern comforts with timeless elegance**. Private yacht charters from **Port de Palma** allow visitors to experience the **Mediterranean in luxury**, sailing along the **Mallorcan coastline** while enjoying **gourmet catering and VIP service**.

Palma's **culinary scene** is equally prestigious, featuring a **mix of Michelin-starred restaurants, exclusive rooftop lounges, and traditional fine dining establishments**. Renowned restaurants such as **Marc Fosh, Adrián Quetglas, and Zaranda** offer **gourmet Mediterranean cuisine**, prepared with **fresh, local ingredients and creative flair**. Meanwhile, the **Santa Catalina district** is a **foodie hotspot**, home to **trendy restaurants, stylish cocktail bars, and the famous Santa Catalina Market**, where visitors can enjoy **fresh seafood, tapas, and Mallorcan delicacies**.

For those seeking **cultural enrichment**, Palma is home to **world-class museums and galleries**. The **Es Baluard Museum of Modern & Contemporary Art**, set within the city's ancient fortress walls, houses **a collection of works from renowned artists such as Picasso, Miró, and Barceló**. Meanwhile, the **Fundació Pilar i Joan Miró** showcases **the studio and works of the famous Catalan artist Joan Miró**, who spent much of his later life in Mallorca. The city's **many independent art galleries, historic mansions, and music festivals** make it a thriving center for **art, creativity, and cultural expression**.

At night, Palma transforms into **a glamorous social scene**, with **chic rooftop bars, exclusive beach clubs, and sophisticated lounges**. Venues such as **Purobeach Palma, El Llorenç Rooftop, and the Hotel Cappuccino Bar** provide **stunning views, handcrafted cocktails, and a stylish atmosphere**, for enjoying **Mallorca's famous sunsets**. The **Paseo Marítimo waterfront** is lined with **luxury nightclubs and cocktail lounges**, where visitors can enjoy **live music, DJ sets, and premium bottle service**.

For those who appreciate **heritage and history**, Palma also offers experiences like **private guided tours of medieval courtyards, VIP access to historic palaces, and exclusive wine tastings at centuries-old Mallorcan vineyards**. The city's **seaside promenades, grand plazas, and charming old-town alleyways** add to the enchanting atmosphere, making it an unforgettable destination.

With its **rich history, luxurious lifestyle, and Mediterranean charm**, Palma de Mallorca is a city that offers **the both worlds**— whether indulging in **high-end shopping, fine dining, and luxury yachting** or exploring its **cultural landmarks, art galleries, and historic treasures**, Palma provides a **world-class experience in the heart of the Balearic Islands**.

II. SÓLLER & DEIÀ (SCENIC & TRANQUIL)

Sóller
Address: Plaça Constitució, 07100 Sóller, Illes Balears, Spain

Sóller is one of the most picturesque and charming towns in Mallorca, nestled in the Serra de Tramuntana mountain range, a UNESCO World Heritage Site. Known for its orange groves, historic architecture, and stunning valley views, Sóller offers a blend of natural beauty, cultural heritage, and traditional Mallorcan charm. This peaceful town has long been a retreat for artists, nature lovers, and travelers seeking an authentic experience of Mallorca's scenic landscapes.

The heart of Sóller is Plaça Constitució, the town's main square, surrounded by historic buildings, bustling cafés, and traditional bakeries. At the center stands the impressive Church of Sant Bartomeu, a stunning Baroque-Gothic cathedral with a Modernist façade, designed by Joan Rubió, a disciple of Antoni Gaudí. The square is a lively gathering spot where locals and visitors can enjoy coffee, tapas, or freshly squeezed orange juice from the town's famous orchards.

One of Sóller's most famous attractions is the Ferrocaril de Sóller, the historic wooden train that connects the town to Palma. Built in 1912, this vintage train journey is one of the most scenic rides in Spain, passing through tunnels, olive groves, and the lush Sóller Valley. The train, with its polished wooden carriages and brass fittings, provides a nostalgic experience of Mallorca's early 20th-century charm.

Sóller is also known for its vibrant weekly market, held every Saturday in and around the main square. Here, visitors can browse stalls selling fresh produce, artisan cheeses, handmade crafts, and local delicacies such as Sobrasada sausage and Ensaimadas (sweet pastries). The market is a great place to experience local life and traditional Mallorcan products.

Another major highlight is Port de Sóller, a beautiful seaside town located just 5 km away, accessible by the historic tram that runs from Sóller to the port. This scenic tram ride takes passengers through orange and lemon groves before arriving at the harbor, lined with cafés, seafood restaurants, and boutique hotels. The horseshoe-shaped bay of Port de Sóller is for a relaxing beach day, boat trips, and sunset dining by the waterfront.

For nature enthusiasts, Sóller is an excellent base for hiking and exploring the Tramuntana mountains. Popular hiking trails include:

Barranc de Biniaraix – A stunning ancient stone-paved trail leading to panoramic mountain viewpoints.

Sóller to Deià Coastal Walk – A scenic hike along the cliffs, offering spectacular views of the Mediterranean and Tramuntana coastline.

Sóller is also home to several museums and cultural sites, including:

Can Prunera Museum of Modernism, a beautifully preserved Art Nouveau mansion featuring works by Picasso, Miró, and local artists.

Balearic Museum of Natural Sciences, showcasing Mallorca's geology, wildlife, and botanical gardens.

Gastronomy in Sóller reflects Mallorcan traditions with a Mediterranean twist. Some of the local dishes include:

Arròs Brut – A flavorful rice stew with meats, vegetables, and spices.

Tumbet – A delicious vegetable dish made with eggplant, potatoes, and peppers in a tomato sauce.

Fresh seafood and paella, especially in Port de Sóller, where restaurants serve locally caught fish and seafood specialties.

Sóller is an ideal destination for travelers seeking a mix of nature, history, and authentic Mallorcan culture. Whether riding the historic train, exploring orange groves, hiking the Tramuntana mountains, or relaxing in Port de Sóller, this town offers a truly unforgettable experience of Mallorca's scenic beauty and traditional way of life.

Deià
Address: Carrer de Sa Cala, 07179 Deià, Illes Balears, Spain

Deià is one of Mallorca's most picturesque and charming villages, known for its dramatic coastal scenery, artistic heritage, and tranquil atmosphere. Nestled in the Serra de Tramuntana mountains, this idyllic village sits on a hillside overlooking the Mediterranean Sea, surrounded by olive groves, citrus orchards, and rugged cliffs. Deià has long been a retreat for writers, artists, and musicians, making it a hub for creative minds and travelers seeking peace and inspiration.

The village is characterized by traditional stone houses with terracotta roofs, narrow winding streets, and stunning panoramic views. The heart of Deià is its main street, where visitors will find boutique shops, art galleries, charming cafés, and family-run restaurants offering a taste of authentic Mallorcan cuisine. The quiet, bohemian atmosphere of the village makes it a place to unwind and explore at a leisurely pace.

One of the most famous aspects of Deià is its connection to the arts. The village became an artistic and literary enclave in the 20th century, largely due to Robert Graves, the renowned British poet and novelist, who moved here in 1929. His former home, Ca N'Alluny, is now the Robert Graves Museum, where visitors can see his writing studio, personal artifacts, and beautiful gardens while learning about his influence on the village.

For those interested in history and culture, a visit to Deià's Parish Church (Església de Sant Joan Baptista) is a must. This small 16th-century church, located at the highest point of the village, offers breathtaking views of the coastline and surrounding mountains. Next to the church is the village cemetery, where Robert Graves and other notable artists are buried, adding to the area's historical charm.

One of the highlights of Deià is Cala Deià, a stunning small rocky cove located about a 30-minute walk from the village. This secluded bay is known for its crystal-clear turquoise waters, dramatic cliffs, and a peaceful setting, making it an excellent spot for swimming, snorkeling, and sunbathing. The cove is also home to Ca's Patró

March, a famous seafood restaurant serving fresh fish and local dishes right by the water's edge.

For those who enjoy hiking and nature, Deià offers access to some of Mallorca's coastal and mountain trails. Some popular routes include:

Deià to Sóller Coastal Walk – A breathtaking 3-hour hike along the Tramuntana coastline, offering spectacular sea views, hidden coves, and Mediterranean forests.

Deià to Valldemossa – A scenic trail leading through ancient olive groves, terraced farmland, and rolling hills, providing a peaceful countryside experience.

Deià is also known for its high-end hospitality and luxury retreats, with boutique hotels and exclusive villas offering stunning sea views and world-class service. The Belmond La Residencia, one of the most famous hotels in Mallorca, is located here, attracting celebrities, writers, and artists who come for its elegant atmosphere, spa treatments, and fine dining.

Food lovers will find a variety of excellent restaurants in Deià, ranging from rustic Mallorcan eateries to upscale gourmet dining. Some must-try dishes include:

Frito Mallorquín – A traditional dish made with fried lamb, potatoes, peppers, and onions.

Tumbet – A vegetarian dish featuring layers of eggplant, potatoes, and bell peppers in a tomato sauce.

Fresh seafood – Many restaurants specialize in locally caught fish and seafood dishes, enjoyed with a glass of Mallorcan white wine.

Deià is not just a destination—it's an experience, offering a unique mix of artistic history, natural beauty, and Mediterranean charm. Whether you want to explore its artistic legacy, hike through breathtaking landscapes, relax by the sea, or indulge in fine dining, this village provides a good retreat from the busy world, making it one of Mallorca's most magical and sought-after locations.

III. MAGALUF (NIGHTLIFE & BUDGET)

Address: Av. de Magaluf, 07181 Magaluf, Calvià, Illes Balears, Spain

Magaluf is Mallorca's most famous party destination, known for its legendary nightlife, beachfront clubs, and budget-friendly atmosphere. Located on the southwest coast of the island, just 15 km from Palma, Magaluf is a magnet for young travelers, partygoers, and budget-conscious visitors looking for an affordable holiday filled with entertainment, beaches, and non-stop nightlife.

The heart of Magaluf's nightlife is Punta Ballena, a neon-lit strip packed with bars, nightclubs, and beach clubs, where the party goes on until dawn. This area is home to some of the island's most famous venues, attracting international DJs, themed parties, and lively crowds. Some of the top nightlife spots include:

BCM Planet Dance – The largest nightclub in Mallorca, featuring world-class DJs, laser shows, and foam parties. It has hosted David Guetta, Steve Aoki, and Calvin Harris, making it one of the most iconic clubs in Europe.

Banana Club – A popular venue offering themed nights, dance floors, and live performances, known for its wild party atmosphere.

Stereo Bar Magaluf – A trendy cocktail bar with a rooftop terrace, for pre-drinks before hitting the clubs.

Oceans Beach Club – A chic beachfront club with infinity pools, sun loungers, and live DJ sets, offering a more relaxed and stylish party experience.

For those looking for budget-friendly fun, Magaluf offers happy hours, bar crawls, and drink deals, making it one of the most affordable party destinations in Spain. Many bars and clubs offer unlimited drinks wristbands, allowing visitors to enjoy multiple venues for a single price.

Magaluf's beachfront location makes it an ideal place for daytime relaxation after a long night of partying. The main Magaluf Beach stretches along the coast, offering soft white sand, clear waters, and plenty of budget-friendly activities. Popular daytime activities include:

Jet skiing, parasailing, and banana boat rides for thrill-seekers.

Boat parties, where guests can enjoy DJ music, drinks, and sunset views while cruising the Mediterranean.

Beachfront bars offering cheap cocktails, cold beers, and snacks.

For those on a budget, Magaluf has numerous low-cost hotels, hostels, and self-catering apartments, making it one of the most affordable destinations in Mallorca. Many budget accommodations are located just minutes from the beach and nightlife, offering convenience without high prices. Some popular budget options include:

Sol Katmandu Park & Resort – A budget-friendly hotel that includes a fun amusement park for guests.

Hostel Floridita – A low-cost accommodation with a party-friendly atmosphere.

Apartamentos Vistasol – Affordable apartments with sea views and kitchen facilities, ideal for groups.

Despite its reputation as a party hotspot, Magaluf has recently undergone renovations and improvements, adding higher-end beach clubs, restaurants, and leisure activities to attract a wider range of visitors. The resort now offers more options for families and couples, with attractions such as Western Water Park, Katmandu Theme Park, and nearby golf courses.

Magaluf is visited between May and September, when the party scene is at its peak, and the weather is warm and sunny. However, for those looking for a cheaper and slightly quieter experience, visiting in April or October can offer discounted accommodation and fewer crowds.

With its energetic nightlife, budget-friendly accommodations, and beachfront entertainment, Magaluf is a top destination for travelers looking to party, relax, and enjoy Mallorca on a budget. Whether you're dancing until sunrise, enjoying drinks on the beach, or taking part in daytime adventures, Magaluf delivers a memorable experience for fun-seekers from all over the world.

IV. ALCÚDIA (FAMILY-FRIENDLY)

Address: Plaça de la Constitució, 07400 Alcúdia, Illes Balears, Spain

Alcúdia is one of the **family-friendly destinations in Mallorca**, offering a mix of **safe beaches, historical charm, outdoor activities, and family-oriented attractions**. Located on the

northern coast of the island, Alcúdia is known for its **shallow turquoise waters, medieval old town, and nature-filled landscapes**, making it an ideal vacation spot for families with children of all ages.

One of the main attractions of Alcúdia is its **spectacular beaches**, particularly **Playa de Alcúdia**, a **7-kilometer-long stretch of soft white sand and calm, shallow waters**. This beach is for **young children**, as the **gentle waves and shallow depth** provide a safe environment for swimming and playing in the sand. The beach is well-equipped with **lifeguards, sunbeds, parasols, playgrounds, and family-friendly beach bars**, making it one of the most comfortable places for parents to relax while their children enjoy the sea.

For families who love **adventure and water activities**, Playa de Alcúdia offers a range of options such as **paddleboarding, banana boat rides, jet skiing, and pedal boats with slides**, which are particularly fun for kids. Boat trips from the port allow families to explore the coastline, spot dolphins, or visit nearby islands such as **Formentor**, a natural paradise with stunning views.

Beyond the beach, Alcúdia's **Old Town** is a wonderful place for families to explore. This **beautifully preserved medieval town**, surrounded by **imposing stone walls**, offers a **fairy-tale-like setting** for a relaxing stroll. Inside, the **narrow cobbled streets** are lined with **small cafés, artisan shops, and historic landmarks**, making it a **delightful place to wander with children**. Families can visit the **Roman ruins of Pollentia**, an **archaeological site** that includes the remains of a Roman forum and amphitheater, providing an educational and exciting glimpse into Mallorca's ancient past.

For an interactive experience, children will enjoy the **weekly Alcúdia Market**, held every **Tuesday and Sunday**. The market is a lively place where families can browse **handmade crafts, fresh fruits, local cheeses, and traditional Mallorcan sweets**. It's a great way to experience local culture while picking up souvenirs.

Nature-loving families will appreciate a visit to the **S'Albufera Natural Park**, Mallorca's **largest wetland reserve**, located just a short drive from Alcúdia. This **protected area** is home to **over 200 species of birds, walking and cycling trails, and peaceful picnic**

spots, making it a fantastic place for **outdoor exploration and wildlife spotting**.

For families looking for **water park fun**, **Hidropark Alcúdia** is a must-visit. This **water park features slides, wave pools, and mini-golf**, providing an exciting day out for kids of all ages. It's an especially great option for cooling off on a hot summer day.

When it comes to **dining**, Alcúdia has plenty of **family-friendly restaurants** serving a mix of **traditional Mallorcan cuisine and international options**. Many beachfront restaurants offer **kids' menus, high chairs, and play areas**, ensuring that even the youngest visitors are well-catered to. Popular dishes for families to try include **Pa amb Oli (bread with tomato and olive oil), fresh seafood, and Mallorcan-style grilled meats**.

Accommodation in Alcúdia is also **well-suited for families**, with a variety of **resorts, holiday apartments, and family-friendly hotels** that offer **kids' clubs, swimming pools, and entertainment programs**. Many hotels are located **directly on the beach**, providing easy access to the sea and ensuring a stress-free holiday for parents.

Alcúdia's family-friendly appeal extends beyond summer, as it remains a great destination **year-round**. The **mild Mediterranean climate**, combined with **cultural festivals, outdoor activities, and historical sites**, ensures that there is always something to do, whether visiting in the peak season or during the quieter months.

With its **combination of safe beaches, cultural attractions, outdoor adventures, and family-focused amenities**, Alcúdia is the **destination for a memorable family vacation in Mallorca**. Whether spending time **by the sea, exploring ancient ruins, or enjoying outdoor adventures**, Alcúdia offers an **unforgettable experience for parents and children alike**.

V. POLLENSA (AUTHENTIC & RELAXING)

Address: Plaça Major, 07460 Pollença, Illes Balears, Spain

Pollensa (Pollença) is one of **Mallorca's most authentic and relaxing destinations**, offering visitors a blend of **historic charm, scenic beauty, and a tranquil Mediterranean atmosphere**. Located in the **northern part of the island**, near the **Serra de Tramuntana mountains**, Pollensa is a town rich in **culture,**

history, and natural landscapes, making it ideal for travelers looking to experience a slower pace of life while enjoying Mallorca's artistic and traditional side.

The heart of Pollensa is Plaça Major, a picturesque town square lined with cafés, restaurants, and historic buildings. This lively yet peaceful square is where locals and visitors gather to enjoy a morning coffee, people-watch, and explore the charming streets of the town. The square is also home to the Parroquia de Nuestra Señora de los Ángeles, a beautiful 13th-century church with an impressive baroque interior and a large rose window.

One of the most iconic experiences in Pollensa is climbing the Calvari Steps (El Calvari), a 365-step stone staircase that leads up to a small chapel, the Oratori del Calvari. Along the way, visitors are treated to stunning views of Pollensa's terracotta rooftops, the surrounding valleys, and the distant coastline. At the top, the panoramic views are breathtaking, making it one of the spots in Mallorca for photography and quiet reflection.

Pollensa is also known for its artistic and cultural scene, attracting painters, writers, and musicians for centuries. The town has a strong connection to the arts, with numerous **galleries, workshops, and cultural festivals** throughout the year. The **Pollensa Music Festival**, held every summer, brings **classical concerts and live performances** to historic venues, adding to the town's **sophisticated and artistic atmosphere**.

For those who enjoy **exploring history**, Pollensa has several fascinating sites, including the **Roman Bridge (Pont Romà), a well-preserved structure dating back to the Roman era**. The **Dionis Bennàssar Museum** offers a glimpse into the life and work of one of Mallorca's most famous painters, showcasing **local art inspired by the island's landscapes**.

Nature lovers will find Pollensa to be an **excellent base for hiking and outdoor activities**. The town is surrounded by **hiking trails and cycling routes**, leading through **olive groves, rolling hills, and dramatic coastal cliffs**. The nearby **Boquer Valley (Vall de Bóquer)** offers a **scenic hike to the sea**, with stunning views of **rugged limestone formations and Mediterranean waters**.

Just a short drive from the town, **Port de Pollensa** offers a **beautiful sandy beach with calm waters**, making it a spot for relaxation, swimming, and waterfront dining. The pine-lined promenade along the bay is for evening strolls, with spectacular views of the sea and mountains.

Pollensa is also known for its traditional weekly market, held every Sunday in Plaça Major. This market is one of the in Mallorca, offering a variety of local products, handmade crafts, fresh produce, and artisan goods. It is an excellent opportunity to experience Mallorcan culture, taste local delicacies, and purchase authentic souvenirs.

Dining in Pollensa is a delightful experience, with restaurants serving Mallorcan specialties in charming courtyards and historic buildings. Some of the most recommended dishes include Tumbet (a vegetable dish with potatoes, eggplant, and peppers), Sobrassada (a local cured sausage), and fresh seafood. The town also has several wine bars where visitors can sample wines from local vineyards, adding to the authentic and relaxed experience.

Accommodation in Pollensa includes a mix of traditional stone townhouses, boutique hotels, and countryside villas, providing visitors with a variety of options for **a peaceful and intimate stay**. Many accommodations offer **stunning views of the mountains, private gardens, and terraces**, making them ideal for those looking to unwind and immerse themselves in the town's tranquility.

Pollensa is a **year-round destination**, offering **mild weather, cultural events, and scenic beauty in every season**. Whether exploring its **historic streets, enjoying the arts, hiking in the mountains, or relaxing by the coast**, Pollensa provides an **authentic and peaceful escape from the busier parts of Mallorca**. It is a town where visitors can **slow down, connect with nature, and experience the timeless charm of traditional Mallorcan life**.

Printed in Great Britain
by Amazon

62910164R10087